VICTORY.
STAND!

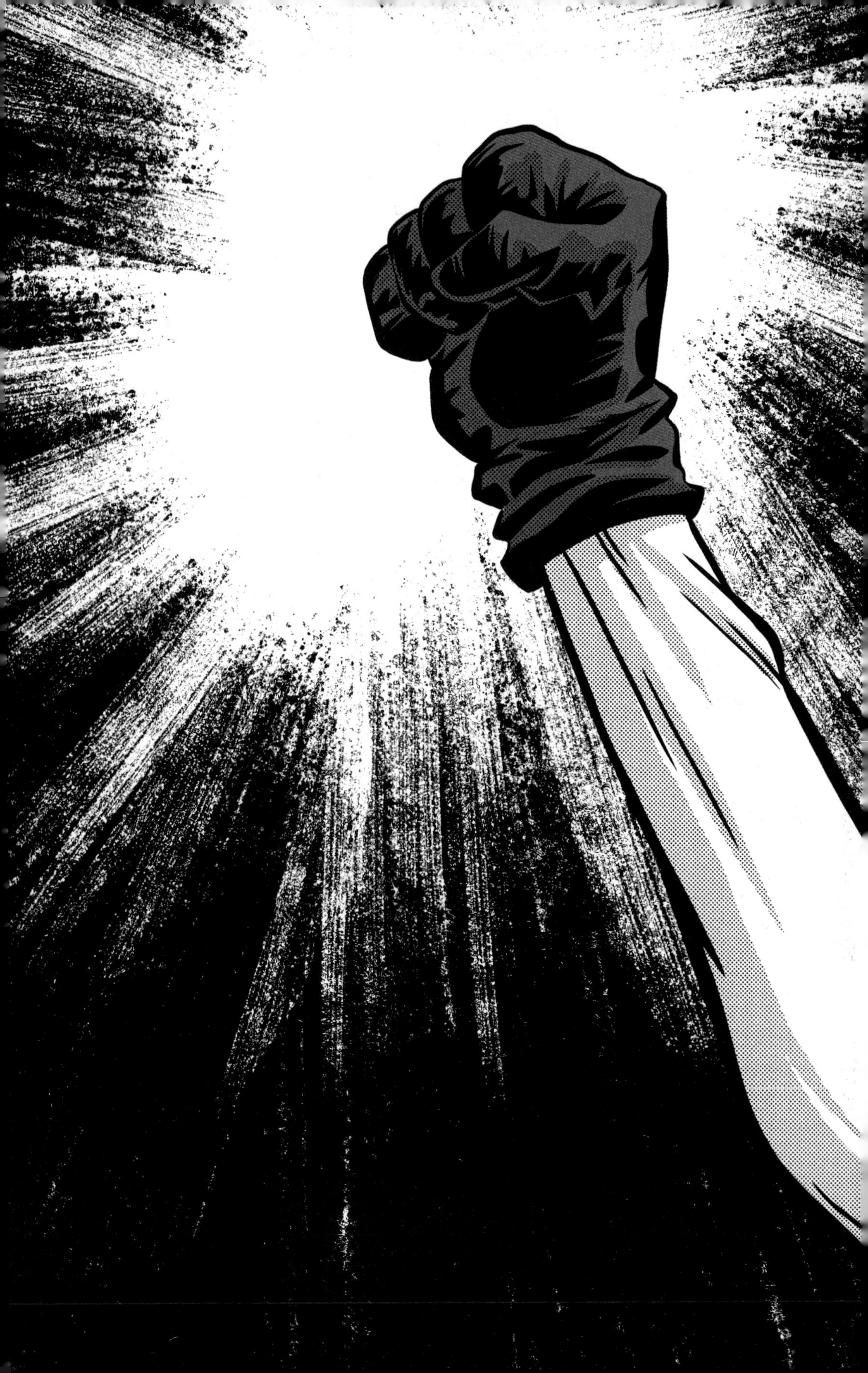

VICTORY.
STAND!

RAISING MY FIST FOR JUSTICE

TOMMIE SMITH
DERRICK BARNES
DAWUD ANYABWILE

NORTON YOUNG READERS
An Imprint of W. W. Norton & Company
Independent Publishers Since 1923

TO MY YOUNG READERS AROUND THE GLOBE.
KEEP THE FAITH, AND WITH ALL YOUR MIGHT—
CONTINUE TO FIGHT ON FOR JUSTICE.
—T.S.

TO MY AMAZING LITERARY AGENT, MS. REGINA BROOKS.
THANKS FOR ALWAYS LOOKING OUT FOR ME. LOVE YOU TO LIFE.
—D.B.

TO HUMANITY.
—D.A.

Text copyright © 2022 by Tommie Smith and Derrick Barnes
Illustrations copyright © 2022 by Big City Entertainment

All rights reserved
Printed in the United States of America
First Edition

For information about permission to reproduce selections from this book, write to
Permissions, W. W. Norton & Company, Inc., 500 Fifth Avenue, New York, NY 10110

For information about special discounts for bulk purchases, please contact W. W. Norton Special Sales at
specialsales@wwnorton.com or 800-233-4830

Manufacturing by Versa Press
Book design by Hana Anouk Nakamura and Max Temescu
Production manager: Julia Druskin

The front cover and section openers of this book are set in Martin, a typeface designed by Tré Seals,
founder of Vocal Type Co. This nonviolent typeface is inspired by remnants of protest signs from
the Memphis Sanitation Strike of 1968.

Library of Congress Cataloging-in-Publication Data

Names: Smith, Tommie, 1944– author. | Barnes, Derrick, author. | Anyabwile, Dawud, 1965– illustrator.
Title: Victory. Stand! : raising my fist for justice / Tommie Smith, Derrick Barnes, Dawud Anyabwile.
Description: First edition. | New York, NY : Norton Young Readers, an imprint of W. W. Norton & Company, [2022] |
Audience: Ages: 13–18
Identifiers: LCCN 2022030776 | ISBN 9781324003908 (hardcover) | ISBN 9781324052159 (paperback) |
ISBN 9781324003915 (epub)
Subjects: LCSH: Smith, Tommie, 1944– —Comic books, strips, etc.—Juvenile literature. | Olympic Games
(19th : 1968 : Mexico City, Mexico)—Comic books, strips, etc.—Juvenile literature. | Track and field athletes—
United States—Biography—Comic books, strips, etc.—Juvenile literature. | African American athletes—Biography—
Comic books, strips, etc.—Juvenile literature.
Classification: LCC GV697.S65 A3 2022 | DDC 796.42092 [B]—dc23/eng/20220818
LC record available at https://lccn.loc.gov/2022030776

W. W. Norton & Company, Inc., 500 Fifth Avenue, New York, N.Y. 10110
www.wwnorton.com

W. W. Norton & Company Ltd., 15 Carlisle Street, London W1D 3BS

0 9 8 7 6 5 4 3 2

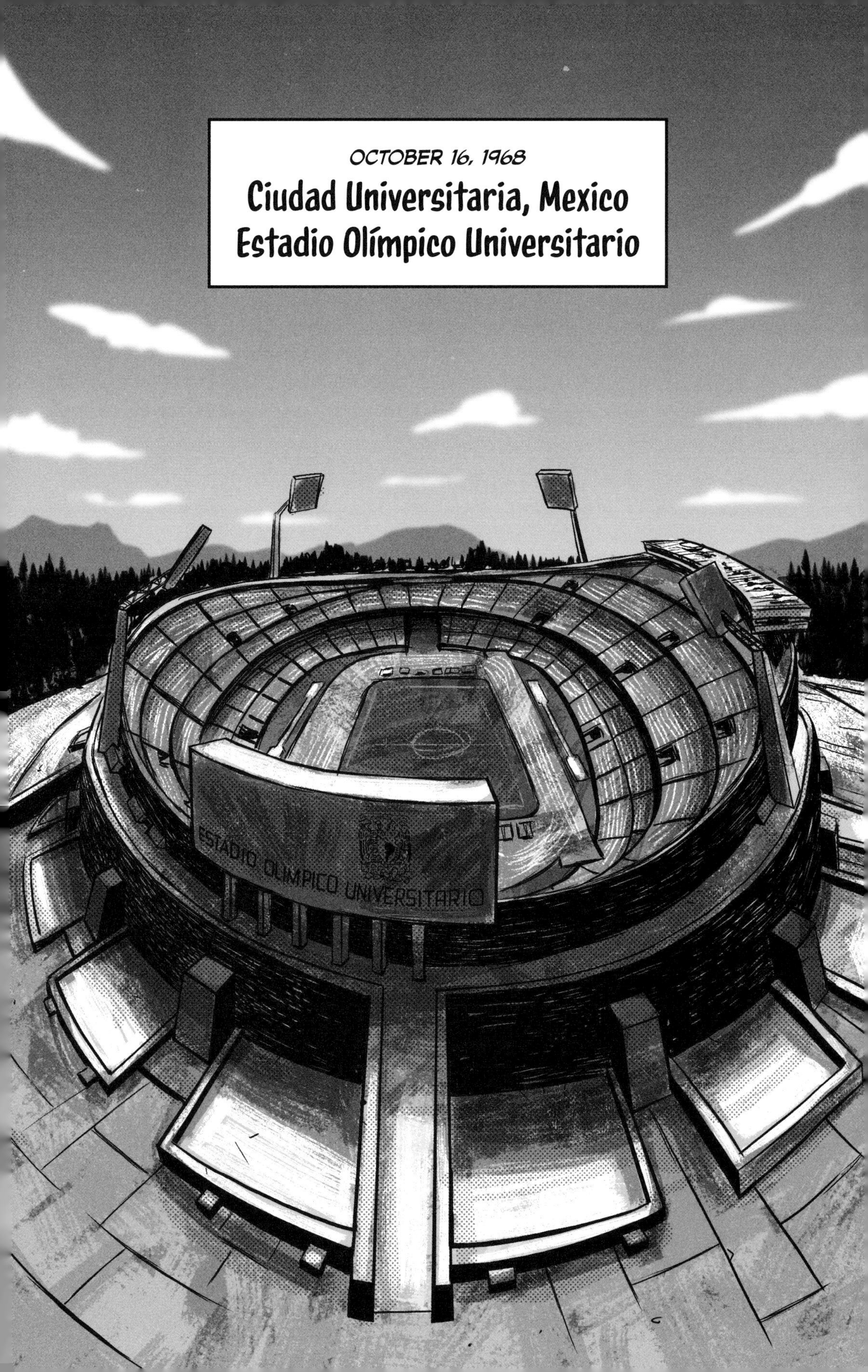
OCTOBER 16, 1968
Ciudad Universitaria, Mexico
Estadio Olímpico Universitario
ESTADIO OLIMPICO UNIVERSITARIO

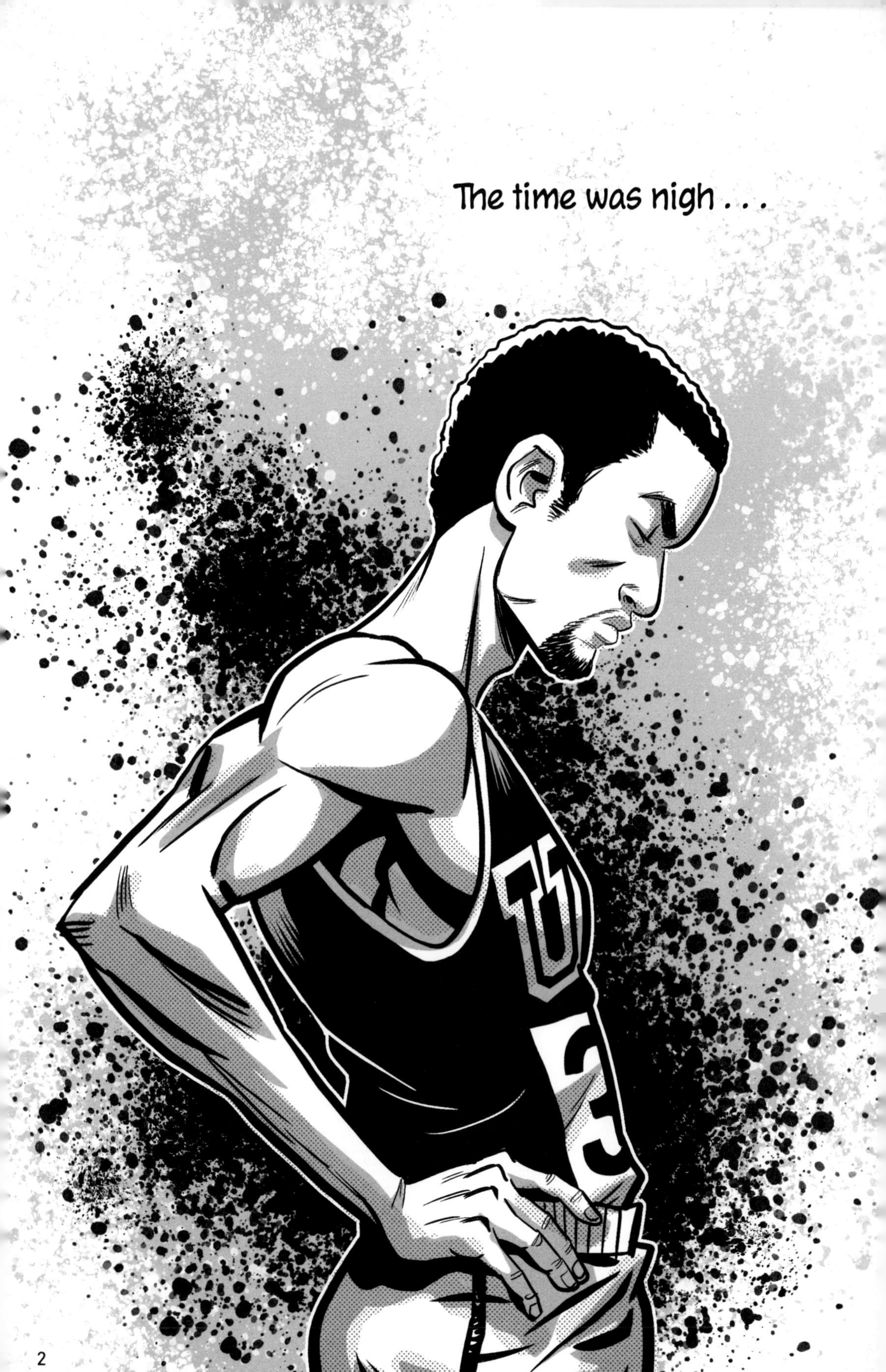
The time was nigh . . .

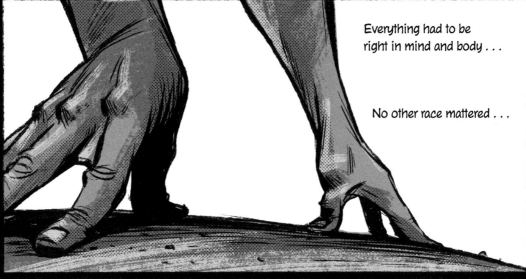

Everything had to be right in mind and body . . .

No other race mattered . . .

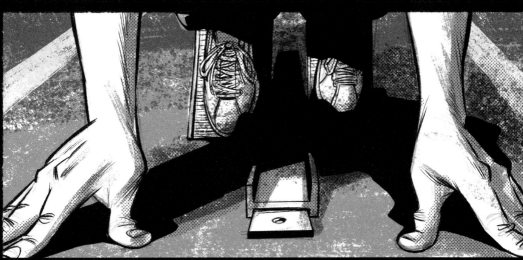

The records, accolades, medals, trophies—none of that mattered . . .

The only thing that mattered was that moment.

There was anxiety, and yes, I was afraid. But most of all, there was determination racing through my veins like ice-cold water.

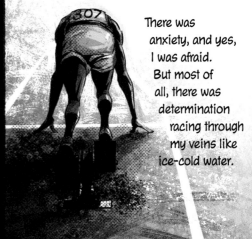

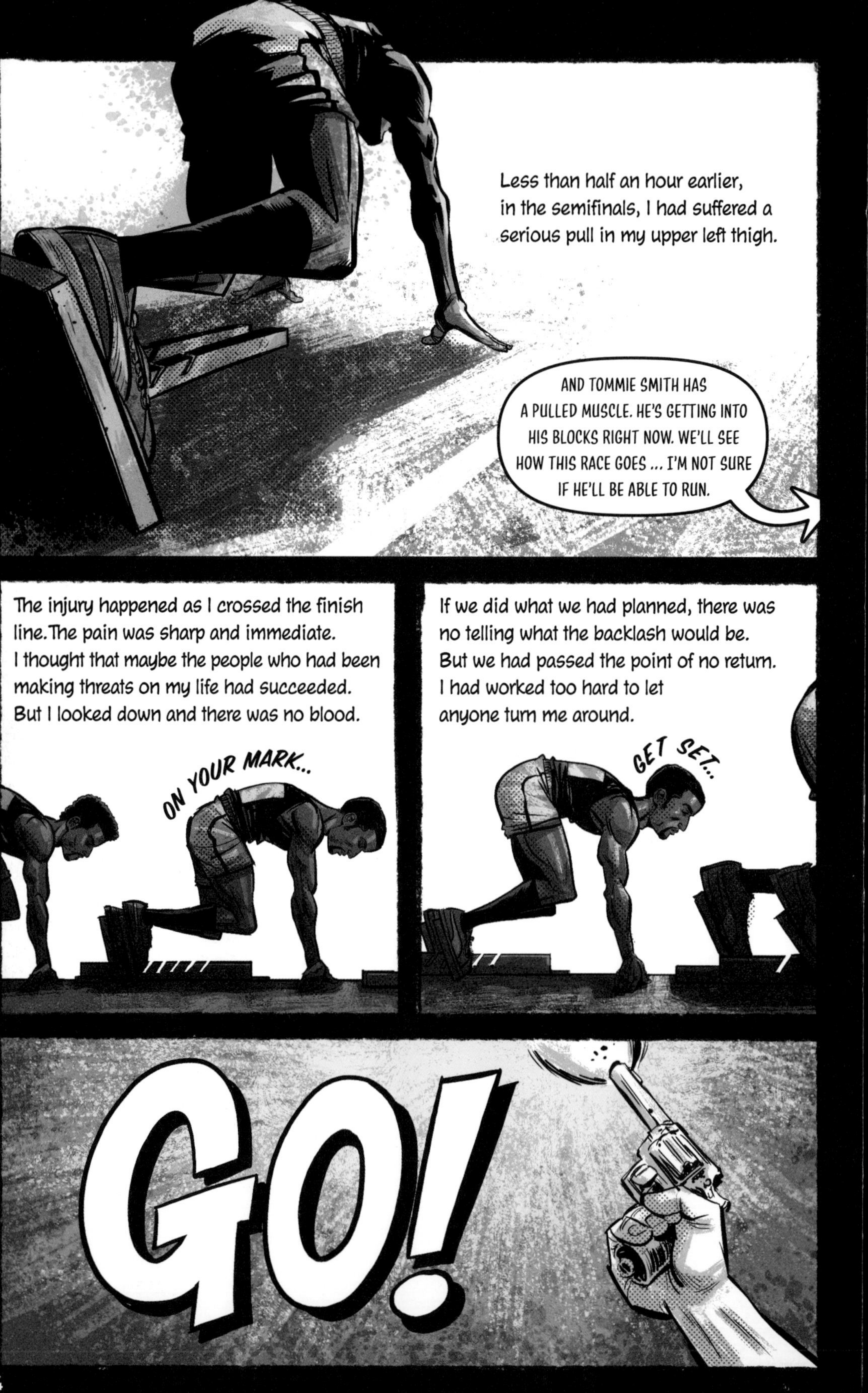

Less than half an hour earlier, in the semifinals, I had suffered a serious pull in my upper left thigh.
AND TOMMIE SMITH HAS A PULLED MUSCLE. HE'S GETTING INTO HIS BLOCKS RIGHT NOW. WE'LL SEE HOW THIS RACE GOES ... I'M NOT SURE IF HE'LL BE ABLE TO RUN.
The injury happened as I crossed the finish line. The pain was sharp and immediate. I thought that maybe the people who had been making threats on my life had succeeded. But I looked down and there was no blood.
ON YOUR MARK...
If we did what we had planned, there was no telling what the backlash would be. But we had passed the point of no return. I had worked too hard to let anyone turn me around.
GET SET...
GO!

Everything went silent at that moment. The only things on my mind were . . .

my forward momentum,

winning in less than twenty seconds,

. . . and whether I had enough strength and speed to outrun a hail of bullets.

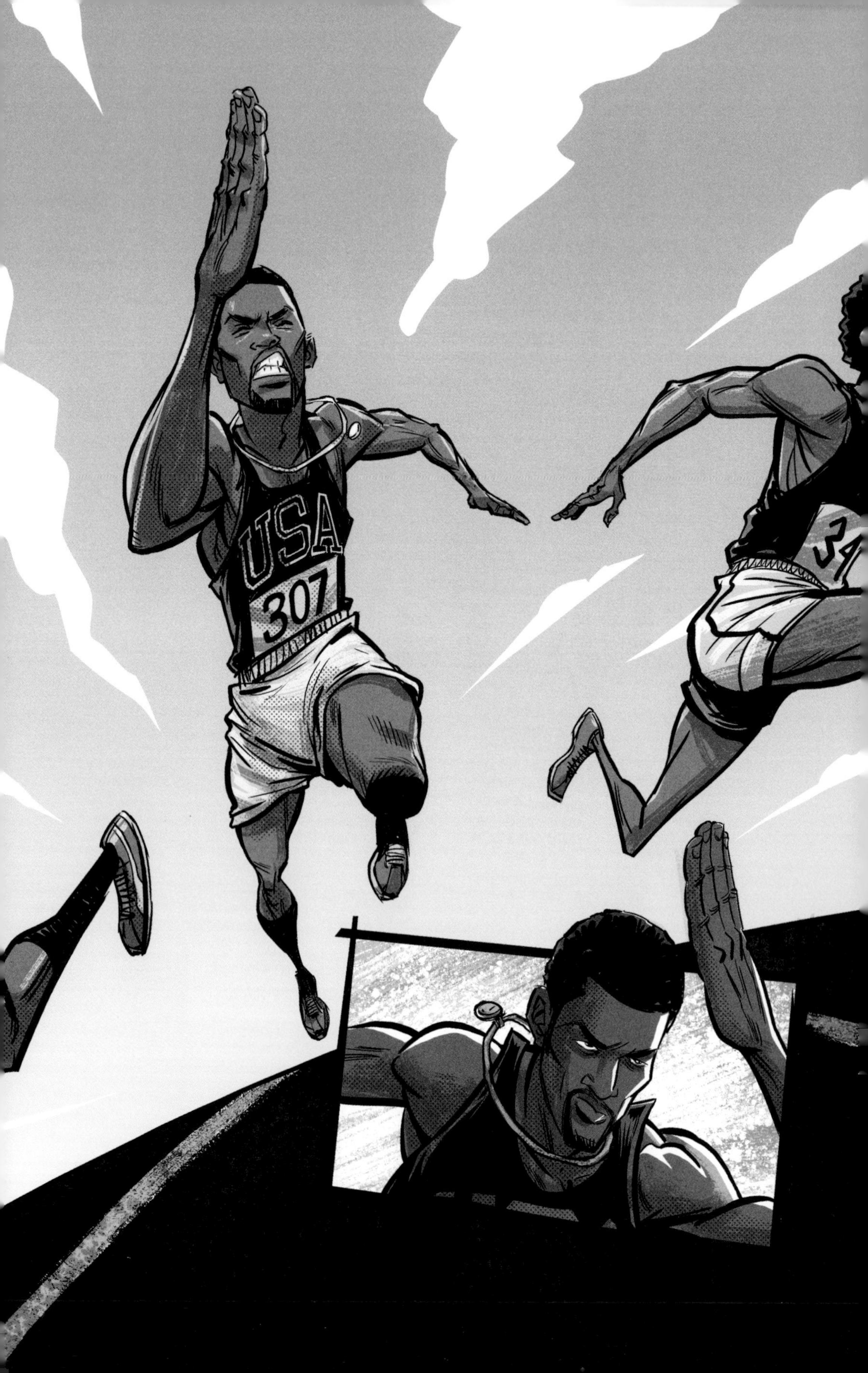
USA
307

CHAPTER 1

COUNTRY BOY

ACWORTH, TEXAS

13 MILES NORTHEAST OF CLARKSVILLE,
RED RIVER COUNTY

REPORTED POPULATION: 20

Probably my earliest memory is of when my father would take us kids fishing.

We'd head through the backwoods, trek through tall grass, and there in the marsh would be dozens of tiny fish, streaking like tiny bolts of lightning through the water.

I'd reach down and try to grab some, but they were always too fast for my little hands.

We were a family of fourteen: my parents and us twelve children.
We were tight-knit, we worked hard, we were plenty, and we were poor.
We were poor—but together we were plenty.

WILLIE JEWEL,

JAMES RICHARD JR.,

GEORGE,

LUCILLE,

THE TWINS SALLY

AND HATTIE,

ERNIE,

MARY,

GLADYS,

"NUDY,"

BABY GIRL ELIZABETH ...

... AND ME. TOMMIE.

Outside our small house, there was no concrete sidewalk or driveway. Only dirt.

There was no running water. No central air-conditioning or heating. No carpet. Wooden walls and floors.

In the fall and winter, Daddy or one of us boys would go out to gather wood and then we'd all huddle up in front of the fire to get as warm as we could before bed.

I was the seventh child.

I was antsy, a bright ball of energy that found it hard to be still.

The only times I can remember slowing down were when I was at my mother's side.

IS EVERYTHING OKAY, MULLA?

In my mind, I was her protector. Against what? I don't know.

She was always so calm and collected, the one we all called "Mulla" and who we all considered the center of our family.

I'M FINE. I'M OKAY, TOMMIE.

Between the cooking, the cleaning, sewing all of our clothes, tending to Daddy, and working the field, Mulla was tired more often than not.

She ached and pained in silence. She was so strong. So kind. So appreciated and loved dearly.

My first job was helping Mulla take water and a pail filled with delicious beans, biscuits with syrup, and potatoes to my father and my older siblings. We had a vast garden on our land. Every vegetable we ate came from the land we worked . . .

land that was not our own.

My father was a sharecropper, which meant he worked land that belonged to someone else, mostly land that had once belonged to slave owners.

My family would work from sunup to sundown and sometimes into the pitch-black darkness of the night, especially when it was cotton season.

There was also sugarcane, corn, and even walnuts. But picking and chopping cotton was how we made most of the money for our family.

When I was old enough to work, at the age of six, I did it all. I helped feed slop to the hogs, helped milk the cow, Ol' Jersey.

But because I was very competitive, picking cotton was my favorite chore.

Especially working side by side with Daddy. It was the only time, as a child, that I can remember ever spending one-on-one time with him. Out in the fields.

My sister Sally and I would compete to see who had the heaviest bag of cotton by the time we were finished.

Sometimes I'd beat her, and sometimes she'd beat me, but nobody could outwork Daddy.

Us kids would take a break beneath a shade tree, and Daddy would just keep right on working. He was serious, and stern, but fair. When he wanted something done, you did it, and you did it the right way.

He would turn over the soil, by himself most of the time, only a single-bottom plow and our two horses, Button and Tom.

If a log needed to be moved or a wagon needed to be pushed, Daddy did it with ease. He was a Black Superman before I ever knew who Superman was.

His stamina and endurance were amazing, and something I drew from later on in my life when I needed a push, when it felt like I just couldn't go on . . .

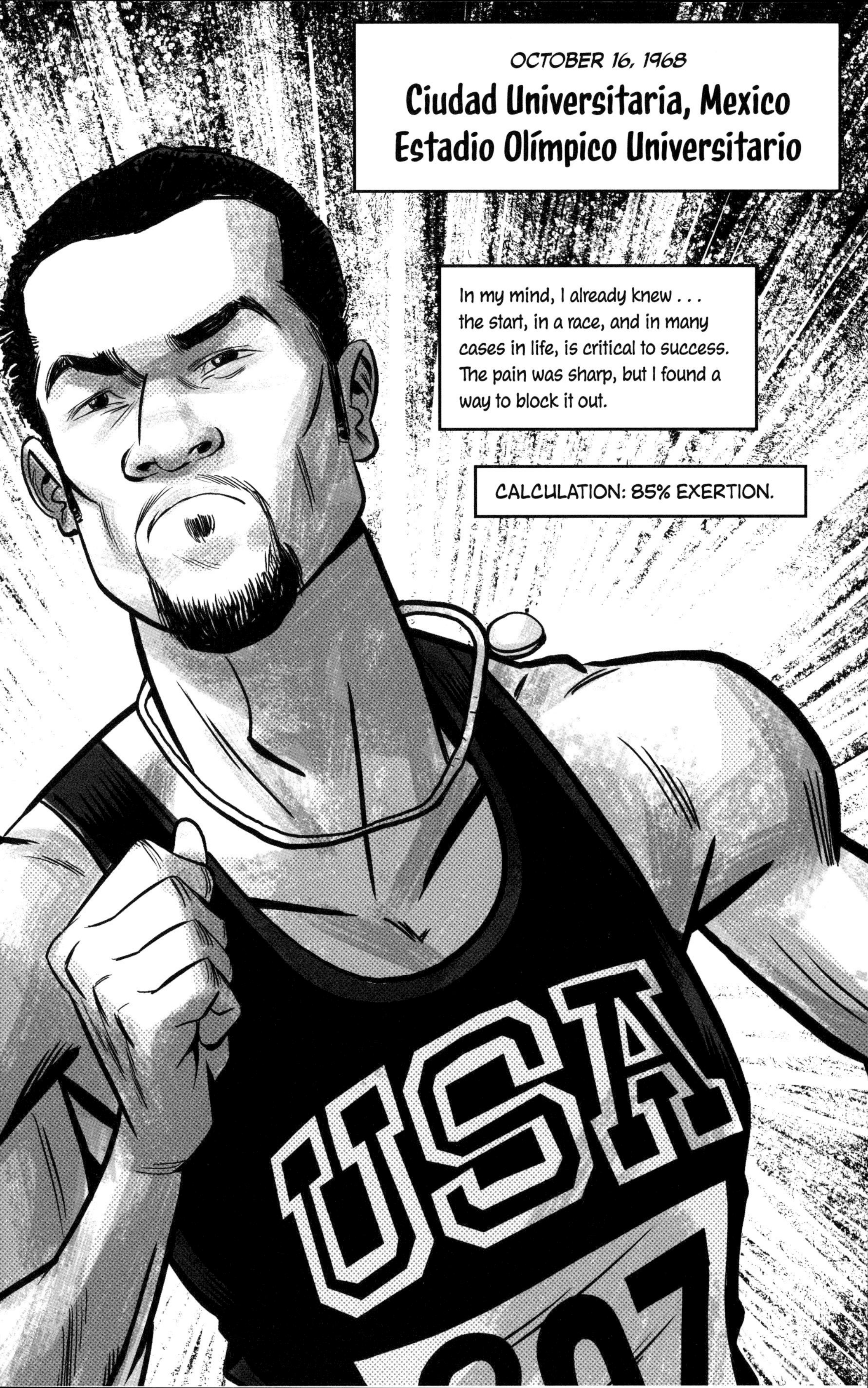
OCTOBER 16, 1968
Ciudad Universitaria, Mexico
Estadio Olímpico Universitario
In my mind, I already knew . . . the start, in a race, and in many cases in life, is critical to success. The pain was sharp, but I found a way to block it out.
CALCULATION: 85% EXERTION.
USA

Being a full meter and a half ahead after the first ten meters would usually assure me of a victory.

But this time, because of the injury to my thigh, everything had changed.

I had to monitor the stress I would apply to the muscle. If I came out of the blocks too slowly or too aggressively, I would fall behind the others, especially my USA teammate John Carlos.

I knew that he would come blazing out of the turn at a full-throttled twenty-two miles per hour. If things didn't go well for me, there would be no catching any of the other world-class sprinters in the race.

Jochen Eigenherr—
West Germany

John Carlos—
USA

Edwin Roberts—
Trinidad and Tobago

Mike Fray—Jamaica

Roger Bambuck—
France

Larry Questad—USA

Peter Norman—
Australia

17

I could feel my pulse, my heartbeat, pounding as fast as race car pistons. My start was smooth, but by mid-turn, I was unexpectedly in fourth place.

How could I muster up enough acceleration to not fall to the back of the pack? For a split second, it felt as if the entire world were ahead of me.

But our bodies are programmed to do what we train them to do. Muscle memory. Consistency and routine had not failed me before. I had no reason to believe that this race, this moment would be any different . . .

It didn't matter if it was scorching hot—Daddy would work.

If the rain poured down and the thunder rang out, echoing for miles across the valley and hills—Daddy would work. Our protector.
Provider.

He and Mulla were our constants.
They set the tone for how we lived, worked, and functioned as a family.

There was no such thing as a "boy's job" or a "girl's job."

My brothers and I swept the floors and helped out in the kitchen.

My sisters fished and hunted.
We learned how to do it all.
All for the sake of survival.

When we were not working, we were making up games to play, like tag, racing competitions, or hide-and-seek within the woods.

And since our nearest neighbors were close to two miles away, on either side, it was only us.

We were all we had.

And as far as our parents were concerned, everything in our lives, great or small, came from one source, and one source alone—our faith in God.

Every Sunday, without fail, my father would hook up our two workhorses, Button and Tom, to the wagon. They'd pull us all, dressed in our nicest Sunday attire, almost three miles to church.

We'd sit still on the "mourners' bench," up front, right next to our parents.

Our church was packed with multiple rows of faithful Black hands, Black hopes, and Black voices.

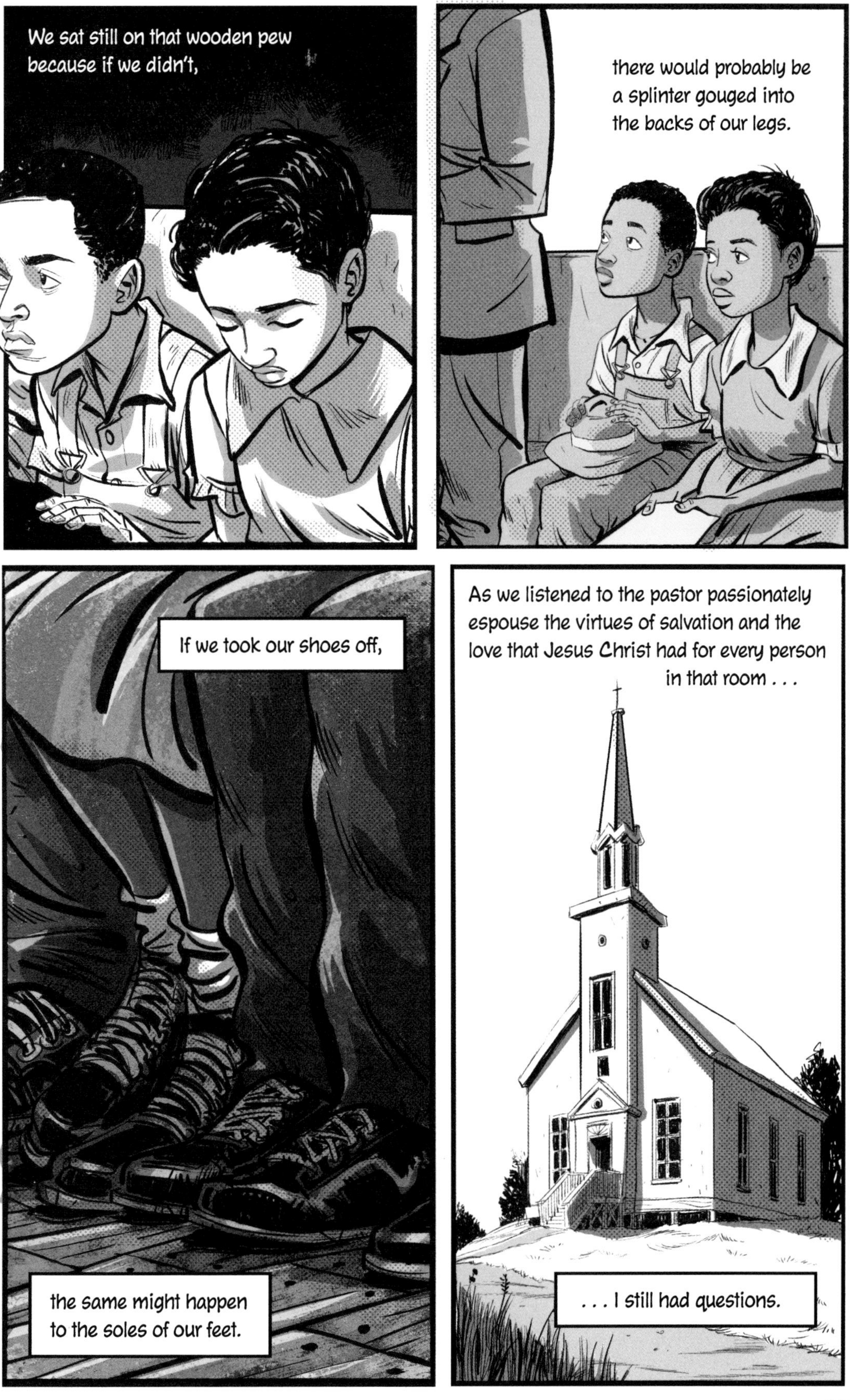
We sat still on that wooden pew because if we didn't,
there would probably be a splinter gouged into the backs of our legs.
If we took our shoes off,
the same might happen to the soles of our feet.
As we listened to the pastor passionately espouse the virtues of salvation and the love that Jesus Christ had for every person in that room . . .
. . . I still had questions.

And even though our parents taught us not to focus on worldly things, only our own efforts and our faith in God,

why did it seem as if they, the white people who owned the fields we worked and the shack we lived in—how come they owned a bigger, better, nicer home? Our family deserved to live just as well as, if not better than, those white families that lived closer to town— closer to the word "nice."

As if you could see it.
 Touch it.
  Just nicer.

We had no plumbing. No running water.
Every drop, every ounce of water we used came from a well.

My mother worked so hard,
inside and outside our house.
The wife of the man who owned
the land—she didn't have to work.

He was the man my father would call
"boss" or "sir" even though they were
both grown men,
men that, in my young
eyes, both deserved
to be called "sir,"
especially my father.

That man's family rode a wagon everywhere.
His children didn't walk to school . . .
wherever they went to school.

We walked to and from
our school every day.

Through the woods,

across a vast, lively meadow,
up and down hopeful hills.

If not for the obstacle course
and natural landmarks,
those three miles
would have felt
much longer.

In our schoolhouse, every grade level from first through sixth was taught by one teacher in one big room on a hill.

Our church was a few yards away from the schoolhouse,

and next to the church was a cemetery.

All three were named Mount Olive.

Only kids from poor Black sharecropping families, like ours, attended that school and worshipped in that church.

And if you were a Black woman or a Black man who happened to work, live, and die in or near Clarksville, Texas, you were buried in that cemetery.

I had no idea exactly where white people were educated or buried.

We would go days, even weeks, without seeing white folks at all. Only when we'd go into town or when my father would go to pick up his pay would we see them.

I had no idea what "segregation" meant, not really. But our lives were all dictated by the separation of those who had and those who didn't.

And those who had not, mostly, looked like me and my family.

I wanted to know why.

But in our home, we didn't talk about race or politics

or why things didn't seem to match up in my mind.

If we were all God's children, why did it seem as if those with fair skin, eyes, and hair were receiving most, if not all, of the benevolence, the favor?

Back then . . .
I prayed that God would provide answers.

Cotton, corn, sugarcane, hogs, chickens, cows, fishing, hunting, school, church, togetherness—

our lives on the land were defined by those routines. So when anything changed, it was very noticeable, especially in my curious eyes.

OCTOBER 16, 1968
Ciudad Universitaria, Mexico
Estadio Olímpico Universitario

CALCULATION: 90%

EXERTION AT
THREE STRIDES
OUT OF THE TURN . . .

I noticed everything that went on around us.

I found it strange that over the course of a few weeks, a couple of months,

our animals had begun gradually disappearing.

I didn't say anything or ask Mulla or my father, but I began to worry that maybe someone was taking them.

And about how we would be paid if there were no chickens to sell, cows to milk, or hogs to raise for slaughter.

Eventually, most of the animals vanished. Every single one except for Button and Tom, our plowing leads, our church steeds.

33

And then, one evening, a big school bus pulled up outside our home.

My father and brothers began to load all of our belongings onto the bus. I knew that we were not simply going on a trip.

As I boarded the bus with the rest of my family

and looked out the window, that little shack in northeast Texas no longer felt like a place we would come back to.

It felt as if we were leaving forever.

The bus was packed with other Black families like ours.
The driver was a white man who wouldn't speak to any of us;
nor would he stop the bus to allow us to use the restroom.
Instead, we had to use jars.

It felt like we were being
transported, like cattle.
Not like human beings at all.

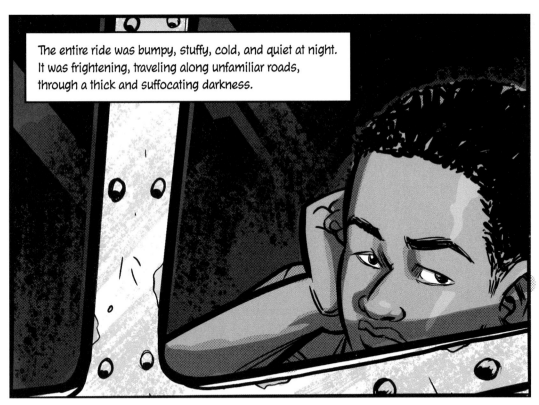

The entire ride was bumpy, stuffy, cold, and quiet at night.
It was frightening, traveling along unfamiliar roads,
through a thick and suffocating darkness.

I had no earthly idea where we were
headed, if we would ever get there,
or why we even had to go.

Almost two days.
More than 1,600 miles.

The packed school bus finally
came to a standstill, surrounded
by a mysterious morning fog that
made it look like the bus was parked
in the middle of a cloud.
And when we got off, it was freezing.
We were not in Texas anymore.

It was the most pivotal move in my
life, and I had no say-so about it.

As lost and miserable as I was then, over the next few years, I began to feel as if maybe—maybe—

God had a plan for me after all.

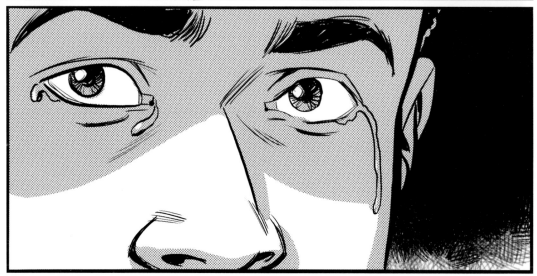

CHAPTER 2

A BETTER LIFE

STRATFORD, CALIFORNIA

CENTRAL VALLEY

Between 1910 and 1970, more than six million Black folks—men, women, and children—fled the rural South. Former slaves and sharecroppers, human beings, escaped:

vicious racism

Jim Crow

lynchings

segregation

the Ku Klux Klan

discrimination

dire poverty

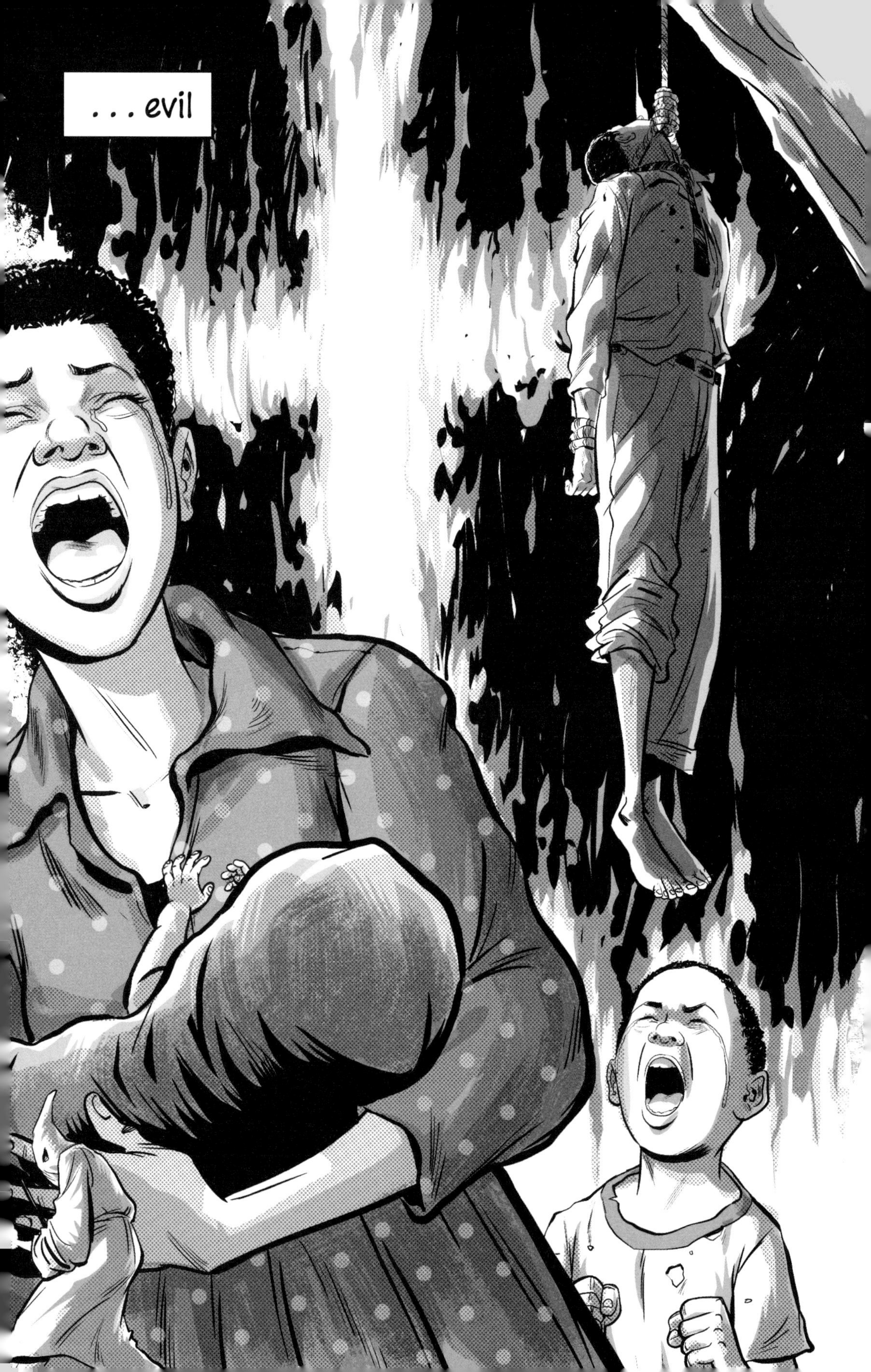
. . . evil

Black folks first went to cities up north, like St. Louis, Detroit, Chicago, Philadelphia, New York, and Washington, D.C. They were looking for industrial jobs.

The drop in cotton prices and the use of mechanized equipment, including tractors and cotton pickers, had taken jobs away from sharecroppers—especially Black sharecroppers, who were making little to nothing as it was.

Before, during, and following World War II, the migration shifted west. This second wave led more than 400,000 Black folks from Oklahoma, Louisiana, and Texas to California.

Three and a half hours north of Hollywood, where dreams come true and glamorous stories were being made for display on big screens all over the world, was the Central Valley,

where my family and I were fresh off that bus, standing in front of a row of dilapidated shacks— our new place of residence, in Stratford, California.

It was called a labor camp.

Every family that lived and worked on that row used the same outhouse or bathroom.

We shared the same place to wash and shower. We did the same hard work that we had done back home.

There were some differences, though, like how everything seemed greener, more lush.

We had cotton, corn, and every other crop we'd had in Texas. And now there were lettuce and grapes—which I hated because of the way the wasps harassed me.

We still didn't own the land we worked.

My parents believed that this move would free us.

Moving to California would open up doors that wouldn't have been opened in Clarksville.

Back home, as long as we were strong enough to work, we worked.

It was as simple as that.

That meant that the children of Black sharecroppers only went to school maybe three to four months out of the year. During planting season and picking season, everyone had to pitch in.

But in our new home, the "Golden State," school was required of all children, regardless of race or what your parents did for a living.

One day, the bus that transported us from the labor camp to the fields came to a grinding halt.

SCREEEECH!

When the dust settled, there was a man wearing clouded glasses, and a suit that had magically avoided collecting one speck of debris.

The driver let the man climb aboard. He stood at the front of the bus, in the center of the aisle, and then introduced himself.

I AM THE HEAD OF STRATFORD ELEMENTARY SCHOOL. IF THERE ARE ANY SCHOOL-AGED CHILDREN ON THIS BUS, PLEASE RAISE YOUR HAND.

Since most of the children were new to Stratford, we responded without consulting our parents. Our little hands just flew up into the air.

I'M SORRY, BUT YOU'LL HAVE TO GET OFF THE BUS AND COME WITH ME. IT'S THE LAW.

My father did not appreciate this strange white man instructing *his* children to do anything.

SIR— MR. PRINCIPAL—MY KIDS AREN'T GOING ANYWHERE. THEY HAVE TO HELP OUT TODAY.

I UNDERSTAND, SIR, BUT IT'S THE LAW HERE IN THE STATE OF CALIFORNIA. TRUANCY WILL NOT BE TOLERATED.

I don't know if my father knew what truancy was, but I'm sure that he knew it was something to take seriously. He was compelled to always do the right things and to adhere to the country's laws, no matter how imbalanced or unfair they seemed at times.

49

And it wasn't that he or my mother were against us kids actually going to school, because they were in favor of it. All they had known, all their parents and grandparents had known, was work. They understood that the only way that Black folks would avoid the seemingly inescapable cotton fields, the now-invisible chains, and laboring an entire day in unforgiving heat was to receive even just a portion of the education that white children were afforded.

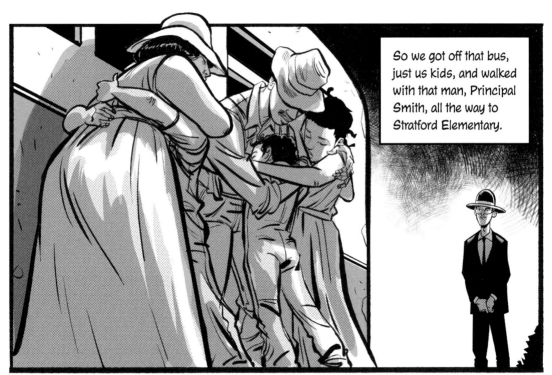

So we got off that bus, just us kids, and walked with that man, Principal Smith, all the way to Stratford Elementary.

My father watched us trek on foot toward our futures. And eventually, he would end up saying to me,

IF I'D HAD THE OPPORTUNITY THAT YOU HAVE, I WOULDN'T BE DOING WHAT I'M DOING NOW—I'D BE DOING MUCH BETTER.

51

That conversation, that one sentence,
echoed in my head years afterward.
To this day.

From that day forward, we attended school regularly.

One difference between the schools in Stratford and the school in Clarksville: we were separated by grade level and not all grouped together in one classroom.

But the biggest difference was that the classes were integrated by race.

It was my first time being so close to white kids my age.

And since I had never been around white students or instructed by white teachers, it was my first time experiencing, firsthand, what "bias"—"racial bias"—really was.

White children were visible.

Apparently, their hands could be easily seen when they raised them, seeking permission to go to the bathroom or to answer questions,

but not mine.

Some days I felt like I wasn't even there.

They had privileges that mattered, like being leaders,

being able to retrieve equipment and balls for recess, and being the ones to stand at the front of lines.

It angered me. It confused me. All of a sudden, at seven, I had to make sense of something that made no sense at all.

After two years in that dilapidated labor camp, my father had finally paid off the debt he owed to the property owners for bringing us to California.

We moved into at least three houses from that point forward. Every time we moved, the house was either bigger or nicer than the last.

One had a humongous lawn, running water, plumbing, a toilet, and a television set.

Finally, we settled in a town called Lemoore.

But between the second and the fourth grades,
between moving off that plantation-like property,

learning how to function and behave, and thrive, and speak properly,
and be, for the first time in my life, among white folks,

and between being a shy kid whose mind wouldn't stop wondering or
wandering and between seemingly growing noticeably taller every week,

there were two experiences that would
foreshadow and help me realize something
that I didn't even know I was really in search of:
what would become of my life.

The first occurred in the second grade at Stratford Elementary.

One lucky morning, my mother gave me a nickel so that I could buy a tiny scoop of "peace,"

a vanilla ice cream cone during lunch.

ICE CREAM

5¢

I held it out in front of me and gazed at a single stream of melted goodness that slowly rolled down the plain cone onto the back of my hand and snaked around my wrist,

like somehow, a chunk of one of those clouds in that California sky that day had fallen to my feet and I'd scooped it up

because I knew that it would taste just like the way my mother had described it: heaven.

But sometimes the worst sort of disturbance can strike without warning.

NIGGERS DON'T EAT ICE CREAM!

He flicked the cone out of my hand, like it was nothing . . . like I was nothing.

SLAP!

I stretched out my little fingers, attempting to rescue that one little speck of happiness.

I watched it somersault to the ground in slow motion. Les smirked with pride.

In his tiny pea brain, he had accomplished something worthwhile.

Even though I wanted to do something violent to him . . . I didn't. I just stared at the cone and watched it melt into the cracks in the soil.

I think I just didn't want to bring any trouble to myself, to my siblings . . .

make my folks look bad.

Hard to say what I was really thinking. I had never been called that name before. It wasn't a word we used around our home.

It wasn't a real word to me at that time at all. It's like it didn't even exist until it was pointed, aimed, and shot directly at me. And I felt it.

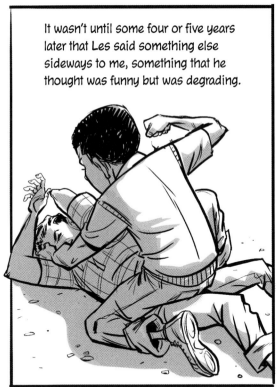

It wasn't until some four or five years later that Les said something else sideways to me, something that he thought was funny but was degrading.

Can't really remember what . . .

but I lit into that boy like a single, lashing flame striking a field of hay over and over again.

There was no holding back. I was willing to accept whatever punishment came my way,

but it never did.

As a matter of fact, I whipped him so good, Les even did some of my farm chores at home.

The second experience occurred when I was a student at Central Union in Lemoore.

Central was the most diverse school I had ever gone to at that point in my life.

There were Black kids, Spanish-speaking kids, white kids, and Native Americans. It was my first time having non-Black friends.

They were all the children of folks like my parents who worked at labor camps.

This experience involved my sister Sally.

Sally and I would race each other back in Texas. She'd beat me, but I'd always be just a shade behind her.

COME ON, TOMMIE. RACE ME TO THE SWIMMING HOLE. THE WINNER WON'T GET BEAT UP ...

Even if I came close to winning, she'd pretend to beat me up, which made me faster.

I loved her immensely.

Sally was in PE class one day, and I could see her from my classroom desk.

My mind wandered a lot in that class because the teacher never let me feel comfortable about being the only Black boy in the room.

"AIN'T"? WHERE ON EARTH DID YOU LEARN TO SPEAK? IT'S NOT "I AIN'T GOT." TRY "I DON'T HAVE." HOPELESS ...

Staring out the window and watching my big sister beat kid after kid after kid was a much better option than pretending to be present.

Apparently, the PE teacher, who was also the principal and the coach of the track team, had grown tired of seeing Sally dominate.

HEY, SALLY, WHAT'S YOUR LITTLE BROTHER'S NAME?

YOU MEAN TOMMIE?

THAT'S HIM. HE'S PLENTY FAST, RIGHT?

YES, SIR.

GO GET HIM!

I watched my sister blaze toward the building and through the side door.

I counted in my head how long it would take for her to get to my classroom. I was right. Four seconds, and there she was.

EXCUSE ME, MRS. YENGER, BUT MR. FOCHT NEEDS TO SEE MY BROTHER RIGHT NOW.

WHAT'S THIS ABOUT?

I'M NOT TOO SURE.

I had never been called on to be excused from class. I knew it was something serious.

Sally nudged me in the gut as we walked back outside to the small patch of grass that served as the playground.

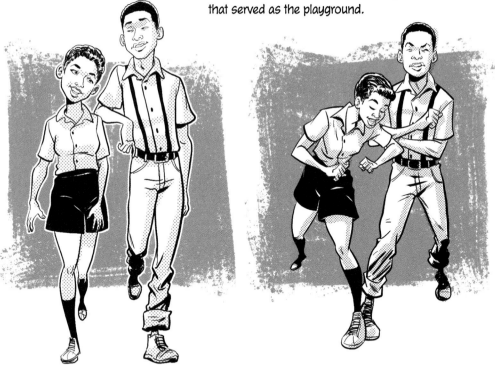

By this time the anticipated race between me, my sister, and the fastest boy in the seventh grade,

a white kid named Coy, had amassed an audience of sixth-, seventh-, and eighth-grade kids.

A small knot began to tighten in my stomach.

69

OKAY, GREAT!
LOOK, KID, I NEED YOU TO RACE AGAINST THESE TWO. LET ME SEE WHAT YOU CAN DO.

When he said that, the little tinge of apprehension in my belly quickly vanished. He looked at me like he knew I could compete.

Even at that age, I took challenges personally. I was a winner. That I knew.

When we lined up I was so tall, it looked like we were all in the same grade.

With that huge crowd watching, and kids pressed up against the windows in their classrooms,

I showed no mercy to Coy,

and absolutely none, for the first time, to my sister Sally.

As soon as Mr. Focht said, "Go!" I left both of them yards behind me.

It wasn't close. Not even.

The cheer of the crowd rang in my ears.
Everyone treated me like I was David. Goliath was every
upperclassman who had ever crushed a fourth grader.

Mr. Focht and Sally's faces
were painted with broad
strokes of disbelief.

It was the first
time I had
beaten her.

I looked up to and loved her so
much. She was a confidante,
a hero. If I could beat her . . .
anything was possible.

The race ignited something in
me, a feeling of invigorating,
unabashed achievement that
no one could take from me.

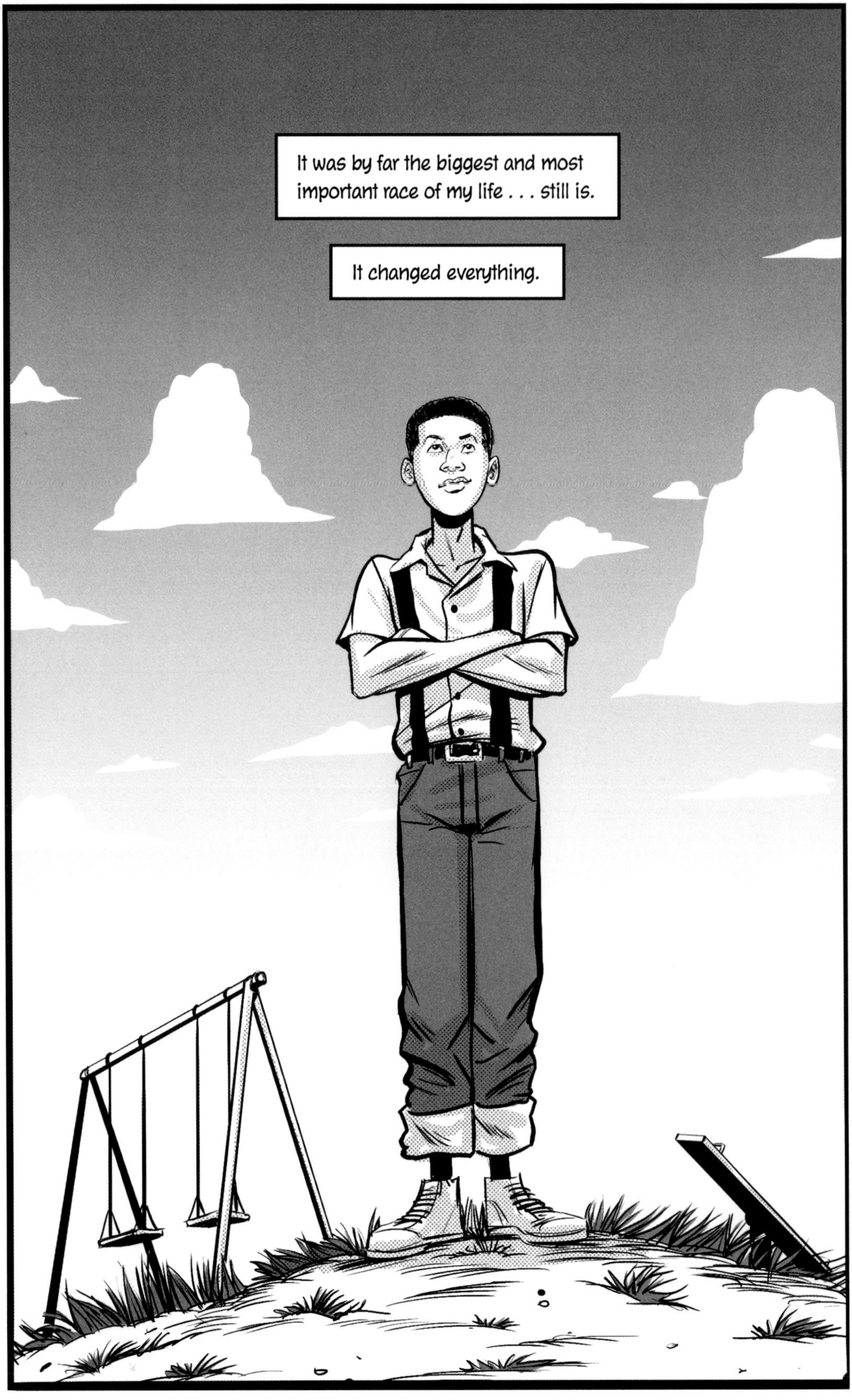
It was by far the biggest and most important race of my life . . . still is.
It changed everything.

Unlike other white teachers at Central Union, Mr. Focht didn't seem to have anything against us Black kids, or any of the other labor camp kids, for that matter.

He was a good man. A really good man, who would help our family out in a huge way.

I DON'T KNOW. I KINDA PLANNED ON TRYING TO MOVE THE FAMILY UP NORTH. PAST FRESNO.

NO, SIR. YOU'LL DO NO SUCH THING.

YOU HAVE A BUNCH OF GREAT KIDS. THEY'RE REAL ASSETS TO OUR SCHOOL. JUST THE KIND OF SCHOLARS WE NEED.

AND YOU ALL ARE JUST THE IDEAL FAMILY FOR THIS AREA. SO I'LL MAKE YOU A DEAL ...

WELL ... THANK YOU, SIR.

YES, SIR. I'M LISTENING ...

HOW ABOUT I HELP YOU AND YOUR FAMILY FIND A BIGGER, BETTER HOME, AND ... YOU CAN START WORKING HERE AS OUR HEAD CUSTODIAN?

MR. FOCHT—I THINK YOU'VE GOT A DEAL.

He did similar things for other families. Working as a school custodian would allow my father to work less in the fields and offered our family more financial stability, which we were grateful for.

Now, my father could not have cared less about me running track.
But when I told him what had happened between Sally and me, he listened.

DADDY ... UM, DADDY ... WE HAD A RACE. ME AND SALLY—AND I WON, DADDY! I WON!

MM-HM. THAT'S GOOD.

WELL, UM, DADDY ... MR. FOCHT THOUGHT THAT IT WOULD BE A GOOD IDEA FOR ME TO—RUN TRACK FOR CENTRAL UNION.

MR. FOCHT IS A DECENT MAN, HE IS ... JUST AS LONG AS YOU'RE STILL HERE TO WORK WHEN I NEED YOU—I SUPPOSE IT'S ALL RIGHT BY ME AND YOUR MOTHER.

THANK YOU, DADDY. THANK YOU!

Daddy went back to what he was doing, and then he stopped hammering again.

TOMMIE—ONE MORE THING, SON.

YES, SIR.

IF I FIND OUT THAT YOU EVER FINISH IN SECOND PLACE—IT'S OVER. YOU'LL BE BACK HERE WORKING WITH US.

YES, SIR.

I thought about two things: how working in those fields was not something I wanted to do for the rest of my life and how, from that point forward, every time I lined up to race anyone, my goal would be to annihilate them.

What he told me lingered in my soul as a source of motivation for the rest of my life as an athlete, as a man . . .

Ciudad Universitaria, Mexico
Estadio Olímpico Universitario

The surge—when your body automatically, without any conscious summoning, kicks into another gear.

It happened to me, that surge, around the eighty-meter mark.

And anyone who was in front of me or who had counted me out was in trouble. Serious trouble . . .

79

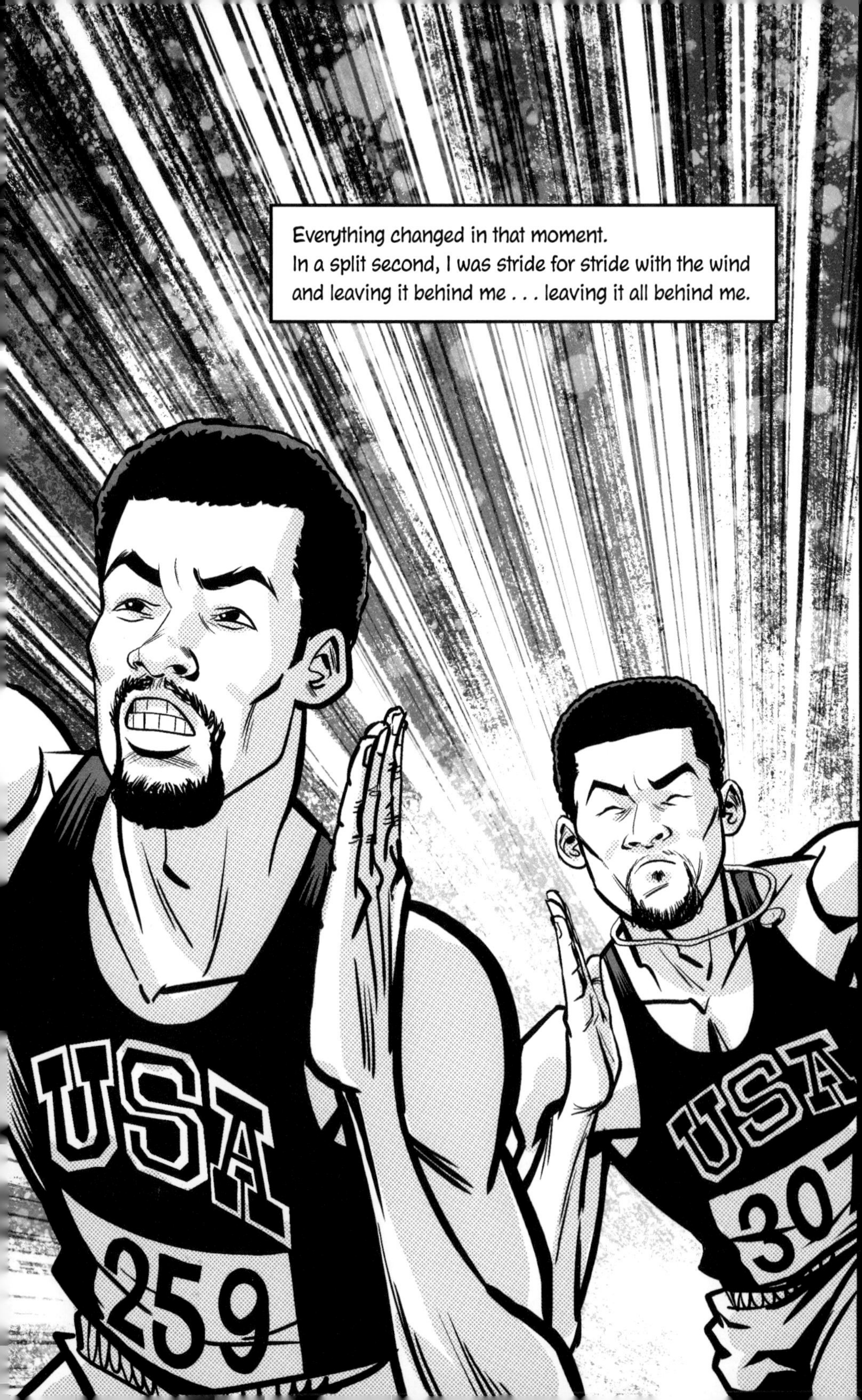
Everything changed in that moment.
In a split second, I was stride for stride with the wind and leaving it behind me . . . leaving it all behind me.
USA
259
USA
30

Although my daddy was a good athlete, he saw no future in playing sports.

There was not a lot of proof that a Black man could take care of his family or make a difference in the world by just catching a football, shooting a ball through a hoop, or running fast.

But when I ran, I was away from those fields. I felt free. It was like discovering a set of wings, racing on a bed of clouds might not be an impossibility.

The team trained after school every day, but I had worked so much in the fields with my father that I was already in great shape.

I ran my first meet in Bakersfield just a couple of weeks after beating Sally.

I blazed out of my stance like a laser beam and didn't even give the other runners a chance.

I won, and I won big!

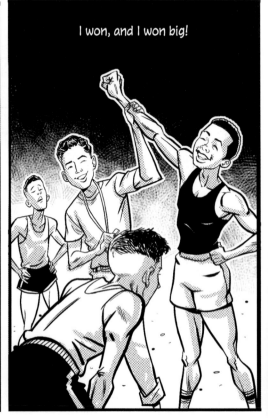

The Amateur Athletic Union gave me a four-inch wooden trophy.

It wasn't my first time winning a race, but it was the first tangible prize I had ever received for doing so—and it was the most beautiful thing I had ever seen.

CENTRAL CALIFORNIA
A.A.U.

1958 Champion
Jr. Olympic
Track & Field

TULARE · KINGS COUNTIES

SPONSORED BY

TULARE   RECREATION DEPT.

I took it home, put it on our mantel, kept it free from dust and harm.

My very first track trophy, and I cherished it.

After that victory, I wanted more, and not just more trophies, but the opportunity to try out other sports.

So for the remainder of grammar school, I continued to run track, but I also played basketball, baseball, and even flag football.

By the time I reached the eighth grade, I was one of the top basketball players in the area, and was continuing to win race after race; plus, I was long jumping like a high school kid, hitting eighteen-foot marks!

But none of it mattered to my parents. Some of my competitions would be too far for them to even consider traveling to. They were simply not interested in seeing me run.

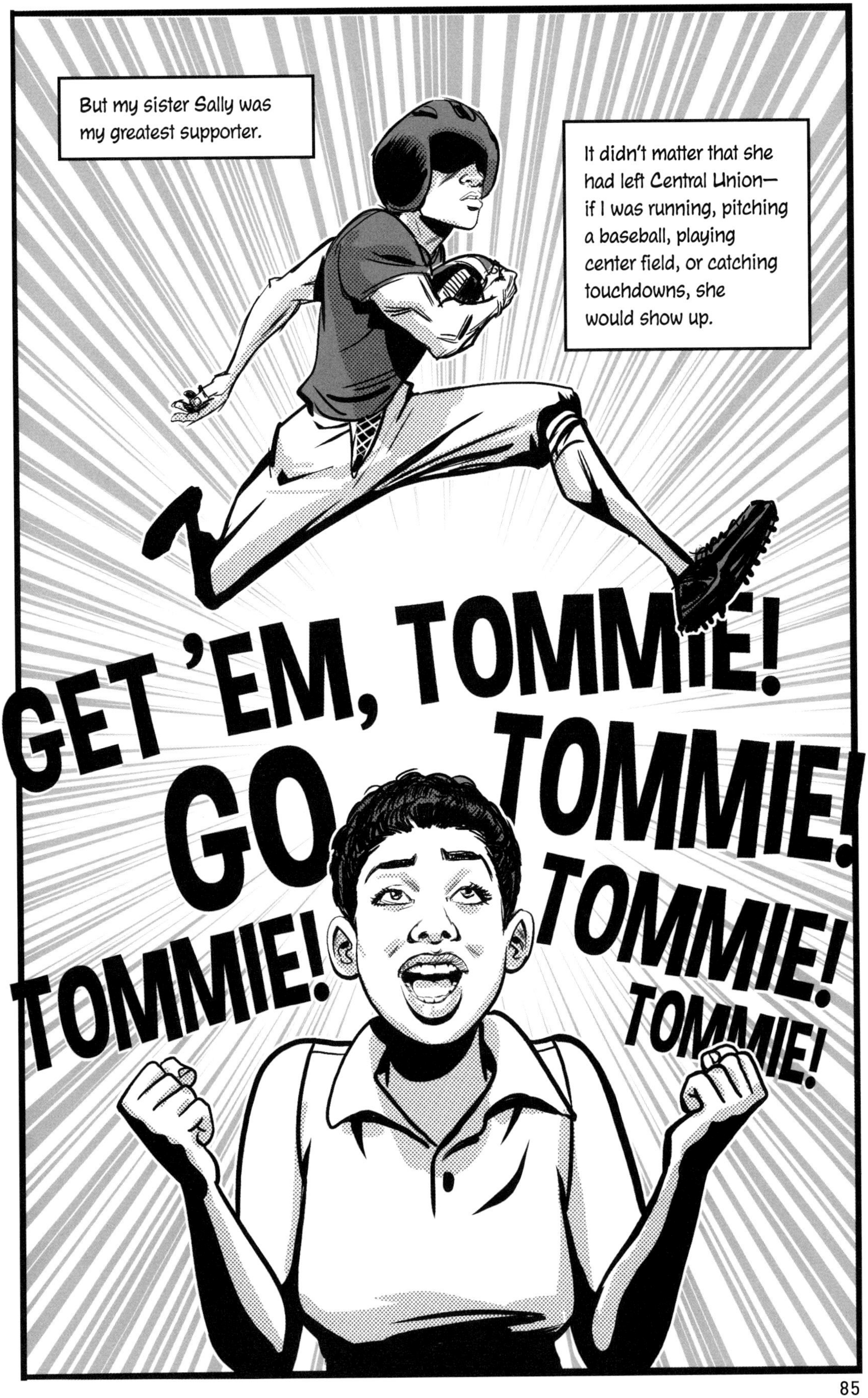
But my sister Sally was my greatest supporter.
It didn't matter that she had left Central Union—if I was running, pitching a baseball, playing center field, or catching touchdowns, she would show up.
GET 'EM, TOMMIE!
GO TOMMIE!
TOMMIE!
TOMMIE!
TOMMIE!

During the eighth grade, I hit a major growth spurt.
I was six foot three and weighed close to 160 pounds.

I was tall and wiry, but I was also strong and fast,
blazing fast—which is unusual for a kid with such long limbs.

It was nothing but God, the reason
I was able to do all of these things.

Nothing but.

In the fall of **1959**, at the age of fifteen, I sparked the interest of every school in the area.

They all hoped that I'd enroll at their school for track, basketball, football—or all of the above.

My parents were still not big on supporting what they viewed as "play" or "games."

All they were interested in was me getting an education. I was a pretty good student at the time. Social studies and history were my favorite subjects.

I wanted to know how we'd all ended up where we were. Why a good portion of white folks in Lemoore viewed being Black as less desirable—as despicable, deplorable.

Sometimes being Black even caused me to view myself, and other people who looked like me, as being of lesser value—not as human as whites.

Mr. Focht continued to look after me, and not as a "thing" that just ran fast and fascinated or entertained white folks, but as a person who prayed, and dreamed, and sang, and cried, and laughed.

He reached out to the coaches of the sports teams at Lemoore High School on my behalf

HE'S A VERY THOUGHTFUL, BRIGHT KID FROM A REALLY GOOD FAMILY.

WELL, I'M IMPRESSED BY EVERYTHING HE'S BEEN DOING.

HE'S MUCH MORE THAN ALL OF THAT. THE KID IS SPECIAL. HE'LL BE AN ASSET TO ANY SCHOOL HE ATTENDS.

I'LL TAKE YOUR WORD FOR IT. WE'LL SEE WHAT KIND OF DIFFERENCE HE'LL MAKE.

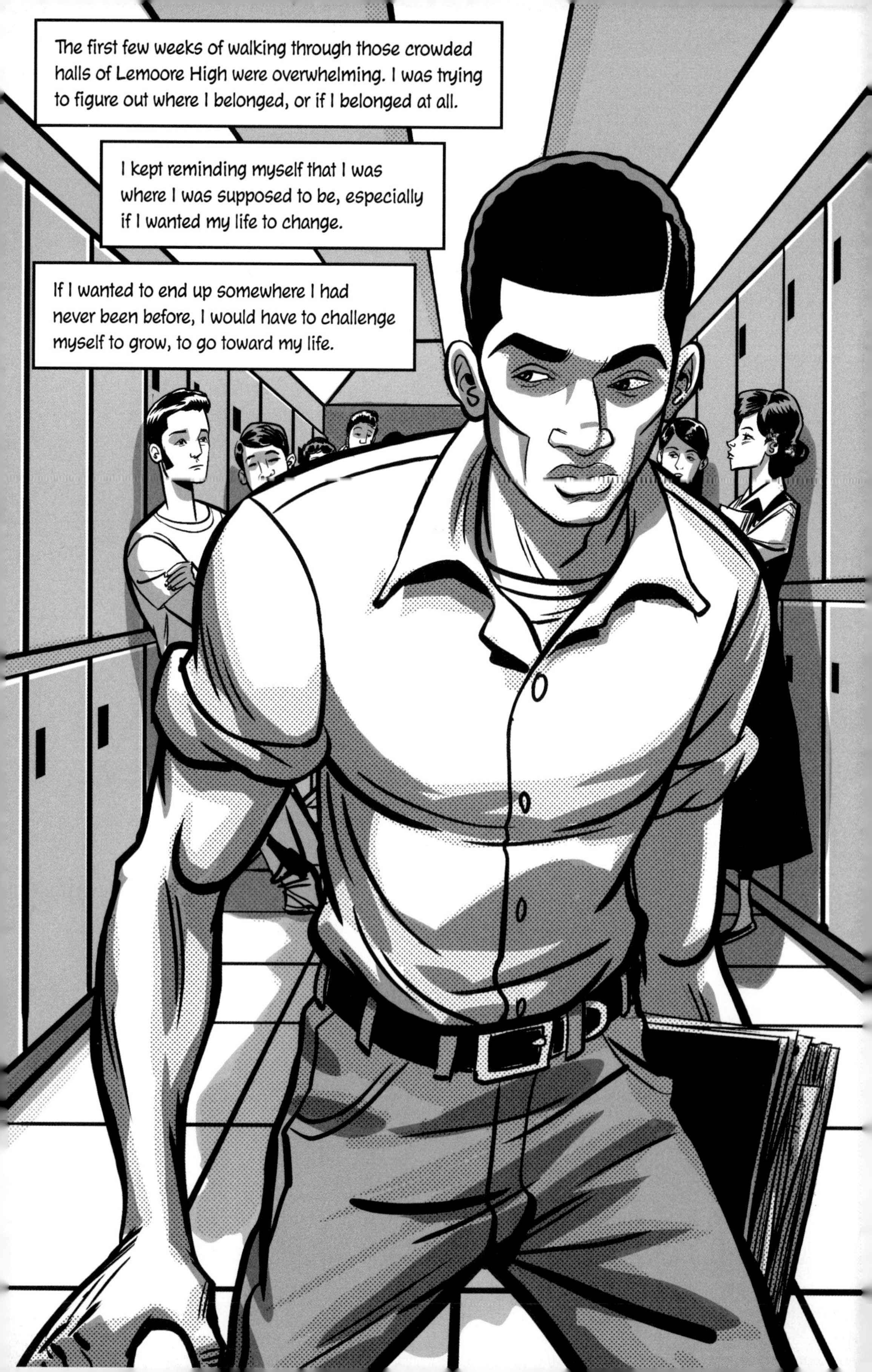
The first few weeks of walking through those crowded halls of Lemoore High were overwhelming. I was trying to figure out where I belonged, or if I belonged at all.
I kept reminding myself that I was where I was supposed to be, especially if I wanted my life to change.
If I wanted to end up somewhere I had never been before, I would have to challenge myself to grow, to go toward my life.

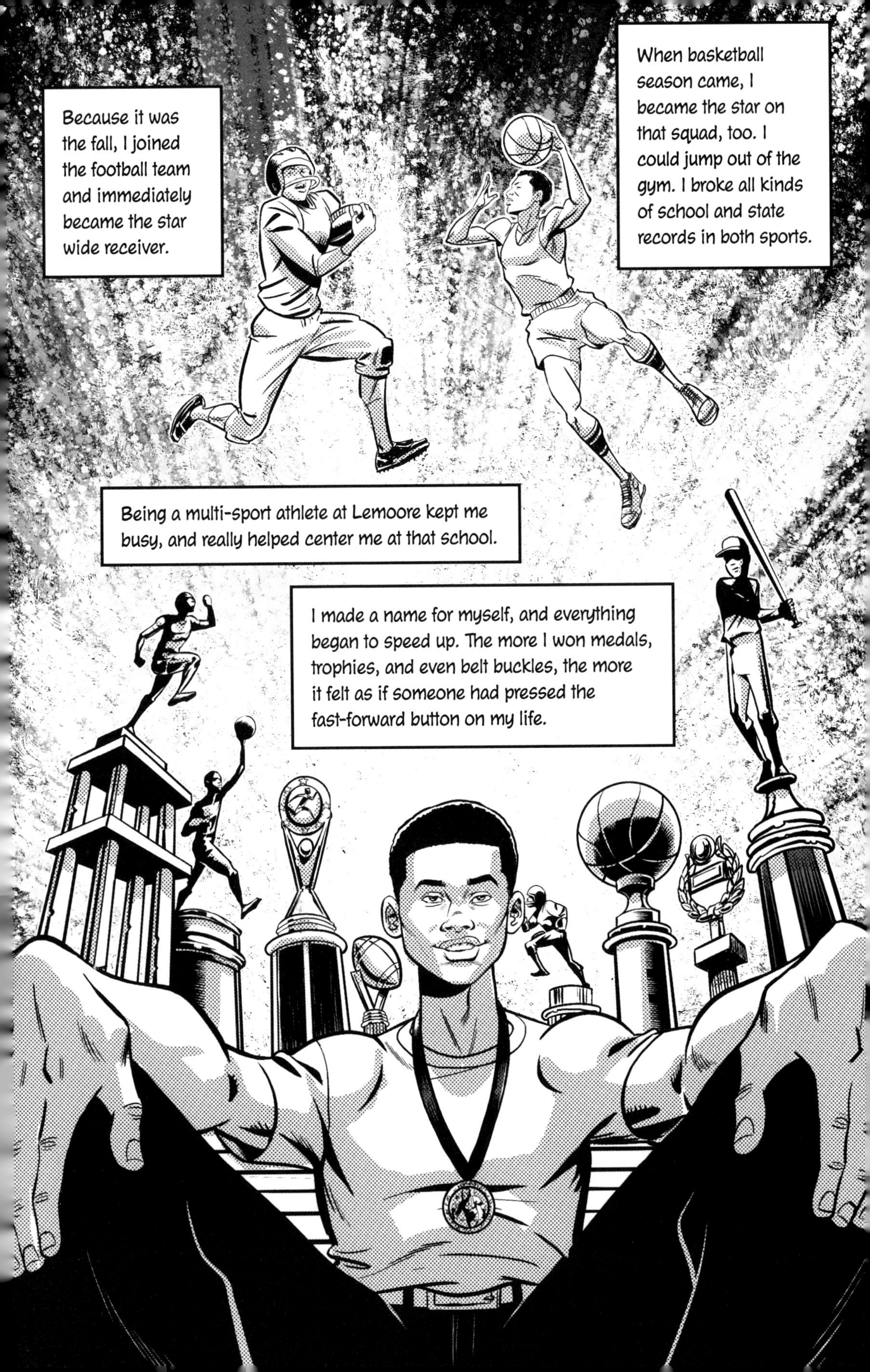
Because it was the fall, I joined the football team and immediately became the star wide receiver.
When basketball season came, I became the star on that squad, too. I could jump out of the gym. I broke all kinds of school and state records in both sports.
Being a multi-sport athlete at Lemoore kept me busy, and really helped center me at that school.
I made a name for myself, and everything began to speed up. The more I won medals, trophies, and even belt buckles, the more it felt as if someone had pressed the fast-forward button on my life.

And even though I excelled at basketball and football, track and field is where I became a supernova.

At every meet, in the back of my mind, I held on to that day on the porch and what my father had said to me about returning to the fields if I finished in second place. I finished first in almost every event I competed in during all four years of high school.

As long as Coach Burton called on me, I was available, and I was always ready.

SMITH, WE NEED YOU IN THE 400 METERS

YES, SIR. GOT YOU, COACH.

SMITH, WE NEED YOU FOR THE 200 METERS, LONG JUMP, AND SHOT PUT

YES, SIR. I'M ON IT.

SMITH, I NEED YOU TO ANCHOR IN THE RELAY AND GET READY FOR THE HIGH JUMP.

YES, SIR.

By the time my junior year arrived, almost thirty scholarship offers had been stuffed into our tiny little mailbox at home.

Some schools were as far away as Hawaii. There were a few in Texas, but I had zero plans of ever returning to that state.

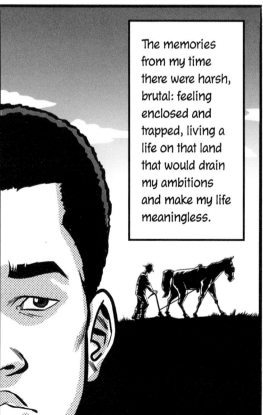

The memories from my time there were harsh, brutal: feeling enclosed and trapped, living a life on that land that would drain my ambitions and make my life meaningless.

And bigger than all of that— I didn't want to be too far away from Mulla, from my family.

In my senior year, the choices were slimmed down to two schools: the University of Southern California, in Los Angeles, or San Jose State, up north.

USC was a big-time, glamourous school in L.A.: movie stars, Hollywood, fast cars, mansions.

The recruiters from USC even brought me down for a visit, but it solidified what I already knew: L.A. was just too fast for a country boy from the cotton and grape fields.

San Jose State was smaller, and my big brother George and big sister Lucille both lived nearby in Oakland. Plus, San Jose offered me scholarships in all three sports and left it up to me to choose.

San Jose State it was.

In the spring of 1963 I graduated from high school.

During the ceremony, the crowd roared and cheered when the many scholarships I had been offered and my numerous sports accolades were read aloud. It felt good to hear about all I had accomplished since arriving on that bus with my family almost thirteen years earlier.

Soon it would be my turn to leave my parents behind, my younger siblings. How would they fare without me? Who would help my father the way I could around the house or when he needed help in the field? Who would look after them?

I felt all of these things. There was a silent tug-of-war happening in my heart.

All I had known was being with my family, working side by side, struggling.

Hand-me-down clothes, not having enough food sometimes, no plumbing, no running water, cold nights, long hot days, leaking rooftops.

When I looked out and saw my mother's and father's faces, it brought all of those moments right back in front of me. I'm sure they were proud. I was, in so many ways, proud of them as well . . .

. . . and it was time for me to go. I was heading off to college in northern California.

Vice president of my senior class.
Arguably the best high school
athlete in California.

And in the same breath,
I was still that little scared, quiet,
skinny boy from Clarksville, Texas,
right near the Red River.

What I would become was anybody's
guess. But leaning on the faith my
parents had instilled in me, I knew
that fear would not get me there.
I was going to be something.
I knew that much.

I worked the fields with my father that summer, and then I moved up north, hurling faster and faster toward my future, like a comet that would eventually collide violently, brilliantly with a destiny I never would have predicted.

CHAPTER 3
METAMORPHOSIS

1963
JUNE

In Tuscaloosa, Alabama, the governor of the state, George Wallace, stands in a doorway at the University of Alabama to keep two Black students from entering.

SEGREGATION NOW, SEGREGATION TOMORROW, SEGREGATION FOREVER.

In Jackson, Mississippi, thirty-seven-year-old Medgar Evers is shot and murdered with a high-powered hunting rifle by a member of a white supremacist group. Evers's wife and children come out to find him on the ground, covered in blood. He was a World War II veteran, an army sergeant who served his country valiantly at the Battle of Normandy.

In Birmingham, Alabama, on a Sunday morning before worship, an explosion kills eleven-year-old Denise McNair and fourteen-year-old Cynthia Wesley, Addie Mae Collins, and Carole Robertson. The first trial for this cowardly act won't be held until fourteen years later. All over the country, Black people continue to catch hell.

I was oblivious to the extent of it. News, via the radio or television, arrived either slowly or not at all. I didn't know it when I said good-bye to my family and left everything and everyone familiar to me, but for the first time in my life, I would be in a position to fill in those empty spaces.

Sometimes in life, the way we see things depends on our point of view.

It was my first time traveling in an airplane. It was a small crop duster, a propeller plane. The flight from the airport in Fresno to San Jose took a little over three hours.

The school had sent me a letter saying that someone would be there to pick me up when I landed.

I had one pitiful-looking bag and was dressed just like a boy who came from the farmland.

My hair was neatly cut. My upper lip and chin were smooth; no peach fuzz.

My ears jutted out like tiny satellite dishes. My sneakers were worn, and my pants were short.

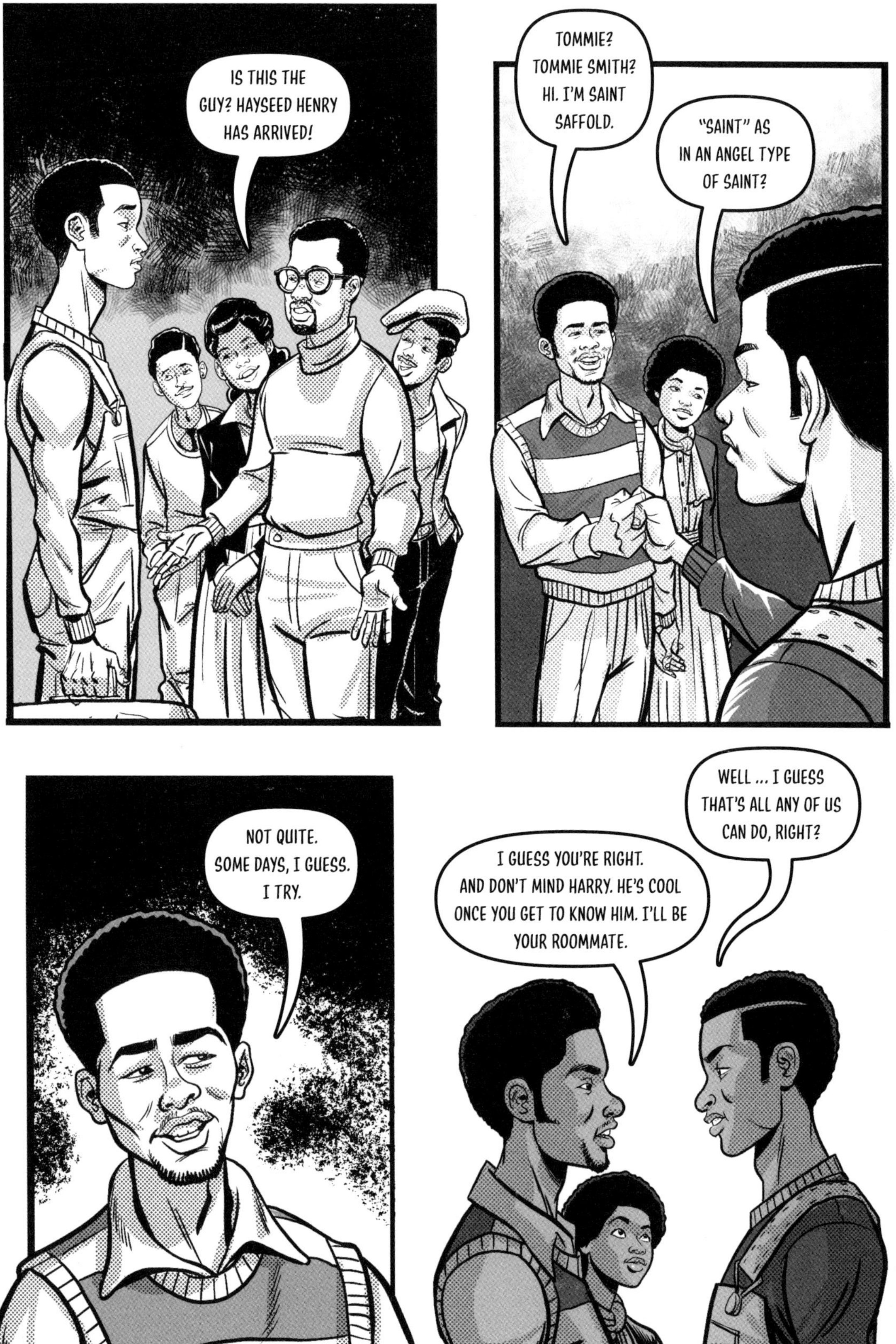
IS THIS THE GUY? HAYSEED HENRY HAS ARRIVED!
TOMMIE? TOMMIE SMITH? HI. I'M SAINT SAFFOLD.
"SAINT" AS IN AN ANGEL TYPE OF SAINT?
NOT QUITE. SOME DAYS, I GUESS. I TRY.
WELL ... I GUESS THAT'S ALL ANY OF US CAN DO, RIGHT?
I GUESS YOU'RE RIGHT. AND DON'T MIND HARRY. HE'S COOL ONCE YOU GET TO KNOW HIM. I'LL BE YOUR ROOMMATE.

Everyone had on the latest clothes, and a couple of kids wore shades—not to block out the sun, but to look cool. They walked a different walk. Although they were not much older than I was, it felt like they were.

I could see each and every one of those kids strolling down Broadway and shopping in Manhattan, or having fancy lunch dates in Paris. Not me.

Saint was the star on the basketball team and played on the football team. But he didn't make me feel bad about appearing to be a country bumpkin. He was nice. Friendly.

As we approached the campus, I saw students, mostly white students, sitting on the lawn studying or walking around, carrying stacks of books.

I thought about my siblings, my father, Mulla. It's not as if I wanted to go home, but I had to remind myself why I was there.

Not to catch a football, not to shoot a basketball, not even to run. I was there for an education. So I could miss my family terribly, but I also knew that if I did what I came to do, I'd never have to work in another field again.

107

When we followed the sidewalks to get to the dorm, it was strange to hear my long, narrow shoes slap the pavement.

The dorm was pristine but tiny, especially for two kids who stood over six foot four. But it was clean, and the mattress embraced me and lulled me to sleep better than a lullaby.

I had a lot to get accustomed to. It was a sensory overload and a definite case of culture shock.

I was already discovering, by the second, who I was. More than just "Hayseed Henry" from the fields.

FRESHMAN YEAR, 1963–64

It was like being a raisin in a cup of milk. I stood out, just like the other twenty or thirty Black students, who were mostly athletes as well.

I towered over almost everyone, as I zoomed in between classes, taking long strides, sometimes carrying five or six books.

White students would stare, jeer, turn their backs, even point at me. They never approached to hold a real, human-to-human type of conversation. Having Black students on campus was still all too new for them.

So—what sport do you play?

I bet you're really fast, right? I bet you can slam-dunk, can't you?!

Do you take—you know—normal classes?

Has anyone explained to you what a major is?

Of course I knew what a major was—
I picked three that first year: music, physical education, and physical science.
But nothing spoke to me like social science.

I wanted to challenge the image of Black student athletes—that we were just there to compete on the school's sports teams, like hired contractors.

I didn't want anyone to come across me and walk away thinking that I was a mindless "spook" from the fields, because that's how they gawked at me every single day.

When I wasn't training, eating, or studying,

I'd spend my free time in the library, doing personal research on the history of America, learning more about who I was, where I came from, and how I fit into the grand scheme of it all.

The library became my second home. I stayed there many nights until it closed.

On the weekend, no matter how tired I was, I woke up on Sunday morning, put on something nice,

and Saint and I would trek across campus to attend church.

I wanted to stay as close to God as possible.

We'd all meet in the cafeteria sometimes— Saint and Harry Edwards,

the other guys from the basketball, track, and football teams. We'd talk about being the only Black students in our classes and share tips on how to adjust.

We'd talk about where we came from, girls, our families, our futures, the unrest happening to people who looked like us all over the country.

I enjoyed those times. It was the closest thing I had to family.

TOO MANY NEGROES IN ONE PLACE AT ONE TIME ... MUST BE PLANNING A REVOLUTION.

I decided not to play football my freshman year. I wanted to focus on my studies, get my bearings. Basketball was my favorite sport at the time—even more than track and field.

Because freshmen were not allowed to play on the varsity team, I had to play with the other first-year students. I was the best player on the team that year.

In the spring of my freshman year,
after basketball season ended,
I went straight into track and field . . .

. . . and during a long jump attempt
at one of my first collegiate track meets,
I injured my hamstring.

But when I healed, I ran the 400 meters in 46.5 seconds,
the best time in the whole country that year—as a freshman.

Working with my father in the fields and cleaning school buildings that summer was my off-season training. I came back even stronger.

I made my mind up that when I returned to San Jose I wouldn't play basketball or football. I had no interest in injuring my legs and risking my sophomore track season, for which I had high hopes.

COACH ... I THINK I'M GOING TO HAVE TO PUT BASKETBALL ON HOLD ...

WHY IS THAT, TOM?

I THINK TRACK AND FIELD, COMPLETELY FOCUSING ON TRACK, SUITS ME BEST.

I UNDERSTAND. I WISH YOU WELL, AND YOU'RE ALWAYS WELCOME TO COME BACK OR TO JUST COME BY.

I immediately went to see the track coach, L. C. "Bud" Winter.

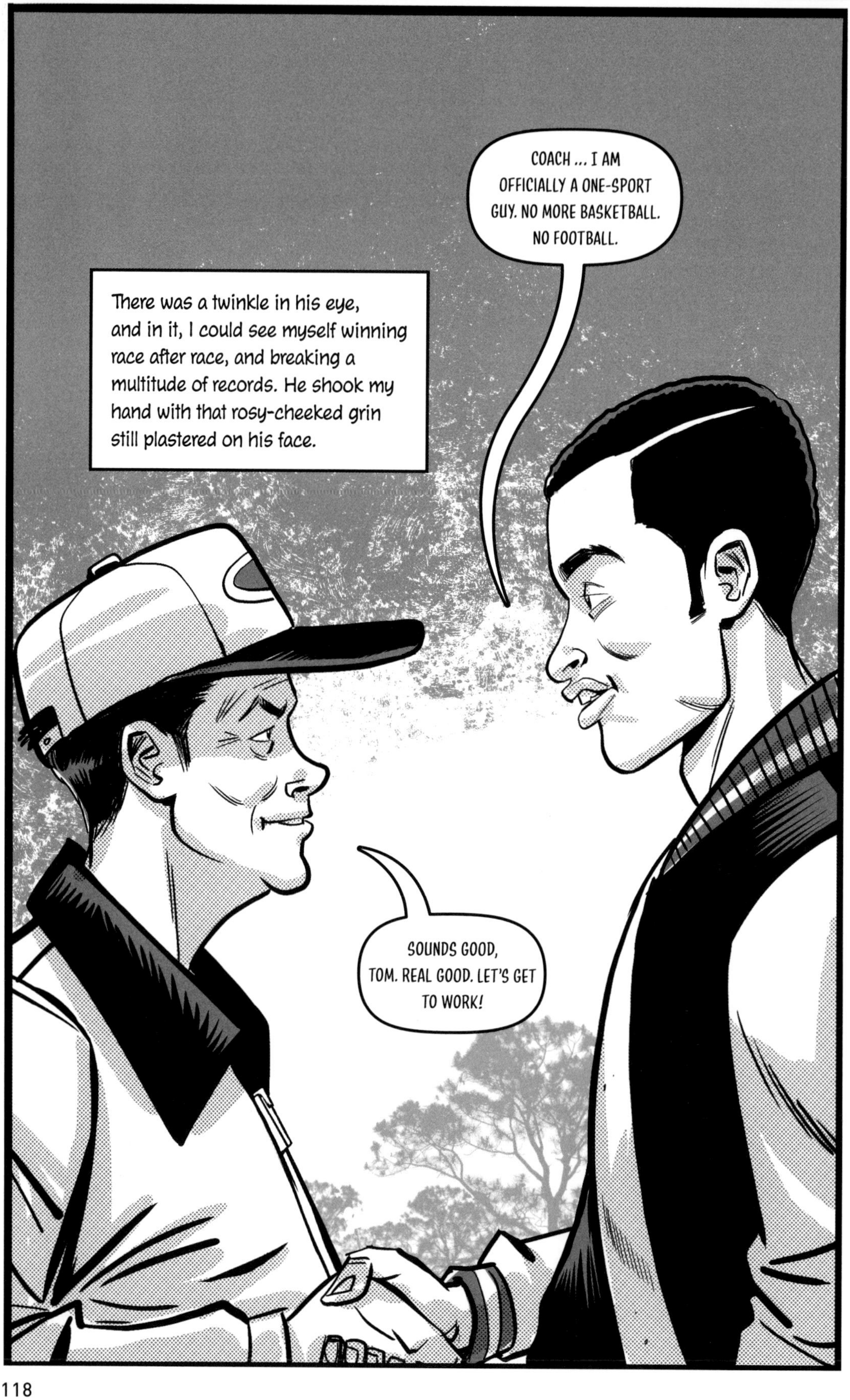
COACH ... I AM OFFICIALLY A ONE-SPORT GUY. NO MORE BASKETBALL. NO FOOTBALL.
There was a twinkle in his eye, and in it, I could see myself winning race after race, and breaking a multitude of records. He shook my hand with that rosy-cheeked grin still plastered on his face.
SOUNDS GOOD, TOM. REAL GOOD. LET'S GET TO WORK!

1964
JUNE

Hundreds of college students from up north, Black and white, travel south to join a campaign to increase the number of Black voters, particularly in Mississippi.

The Ku Klux Klan threatens the lives of any Black person registering to vote—and anyone believed to be assisting them.

Three of those young people, Michael Schwerner, Andrew Goodman, and James Chaney, go missing. Absolutely disappear.

Two months later, their bodies are discovered in a shallow grave in Neshoba County, Mississippi. They had all been shot at close range. An investigation later finds that members of the KKK and the local police force had been involved. The three men are martyrs for what is called the "Freedom Summer."

SOPHOMORE YEAR, 1964–65

At first glance, you would not believe that Coach Winter knew a thing about coaching world-class athletes. He looked more like your slightly pudgy, extremely nice, humorous uncle.

He didn't yell and scream. He had one of the coolest, liveliest laughs you'd ever hear. He would wear his fishing clothes to track practice sometimes.

But the man had been the head track and field coach at San Jose since 1941. He had already, by the time I arrived, trained so many world-class athletes that in 1956 his squad earned the name "Speed City."

I not only wanted to be a part of Speed City, I wanted to be its fastest member—ever.

120

He viewed the human body sort of like it was a machine that could be controlled by the mind, by science.

LET'S GET IT, TOMMIE. I BELIEVE IN YOU GUYS.

FLIP THOSE ANKLES. HIGH KNEES, TOM. HIGH KNEES!

SURE OUR WORKOUTS ARE TOUGH, BUT YOU'RE TOUGHER MEN. YES, YOU ARE!

KEEP THOSE ANTAGONISTIC MUSCLES RELAXED. DON'T LET THEM TENSE UP ON YOU. LET THAT MEAT HANG ON THE BONES!

LET'S HAVE GOOD ARM ACTION, AND KEEP YOUR HANDS LOOSE, GUYS.

It didn't matter what weakness a runner had. Coach Winter could always find a way to get the most out of the guy.

He was genuine and honest, and I knew that I could learn a lot from him. The sky was the limit. With Coach Winter, I was discovering who I could become on the track. And what I was becoming was a force to be reckoned with.

At the time, campus was buzzing with talk of a march to support the brothers and sisters in Mississippi, Louisiana, and Georgia. Flyers were plastered everywhere.

1965
MARCH 7

Twenty-five-year-old John Lewis and other pastors and civil rights activists lead a group of six hundred marchers from Selma, Alabama, heading to Montgomery.

They are protesting the murder of an unarmed deacon from Marion, Alabama, named Jimmie Lee Jackson. Mr. Jackson had been leading a peaceful voters' rights march when he was beaten and shot to death by state troopers.

John Lewis and those six hundred innocent men, women, and teens are met at the Edmund Pettus Bridge by policemen wielding nightsticks. Many of the marchers are hospitalized. The whole event is captured on television for the world to see—including those of us in San Jose, California . . .

The sympathy march was set to happen on the same day as a track meet where Coach Winter and I had talked about me breaking a record. The dilemma for me was whether to run in the meet or participate fully in the demonstration.

I prayed and asked for guidance.

It was a small meet on the San Jose campus that involved UC Santa Barbara, San Jose State (Speed City), and University of the Pacific, in Stockton.

We ran on a track made of graveled, fragmented lava called cinder. I had already visualized myself running so fast that flames would sear and spark from the soles of my feet.

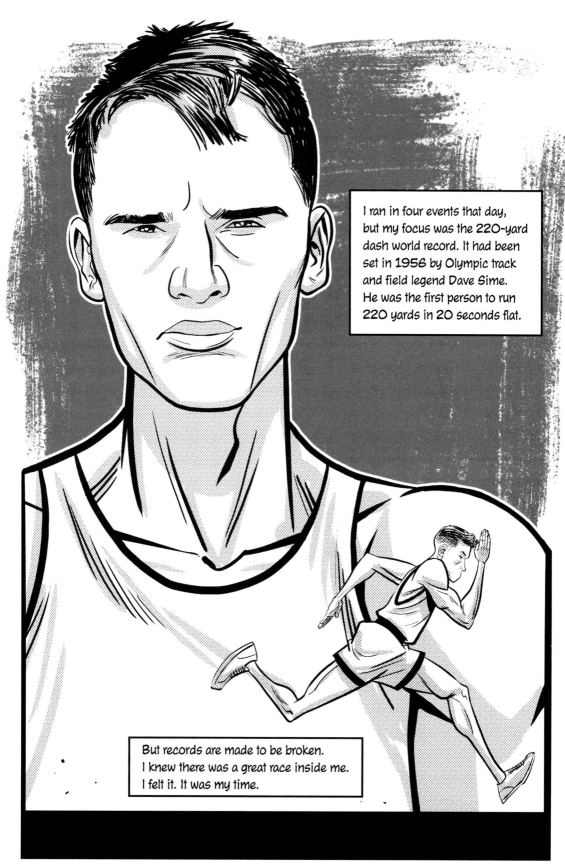

I ran in four events that day, but my focus was the 220-yard dash world record. It had been set in 1956 by Olympic track and field legend Dave Sime. He was the first person to run 220 yards in 20 seconds flat.

But records are made to be broken. I knew there was a great race inside me. I felt it. It was my time.

All week before the race, I focused on getting out of the blocks. And because it was a straightaway track, I had to program my mind and body to finish exceptionally strong. Every single stride was important.

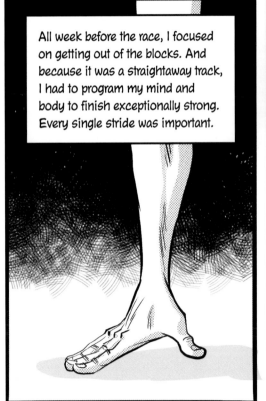

Because of Coach Winter, I had begun to look at my body as if it were an automobile. Shifting power between muscles was an ability I had begun to master.

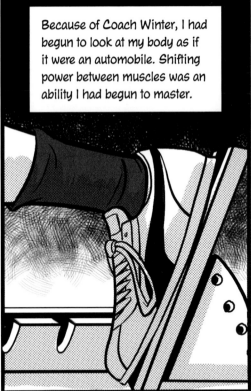

USE THE SCIENCE TO YOUR BENEFIT, TOM-TOM. NO HEAD MOVEMENT ... FORELEG STRETCH ... HIGH KNEES ... HAND MOVEMENT AND ARM ACTION ...

That was it. Coach Winter never talked to me much before meets. He respected my space and the time I needed to mentally prepare.

When the starter pistol sounded, I didn't come out of the blocks as strong as I could've. But I recovered. In fact, my first 70 or so yards were the fastest I had run.

All I could hear was the whizzing of the wind past my ears.

The other runners began to disappear, one by one, as if they had never left the starting blocks.

The spectators in the stands became one long blur of faces and waving arms.

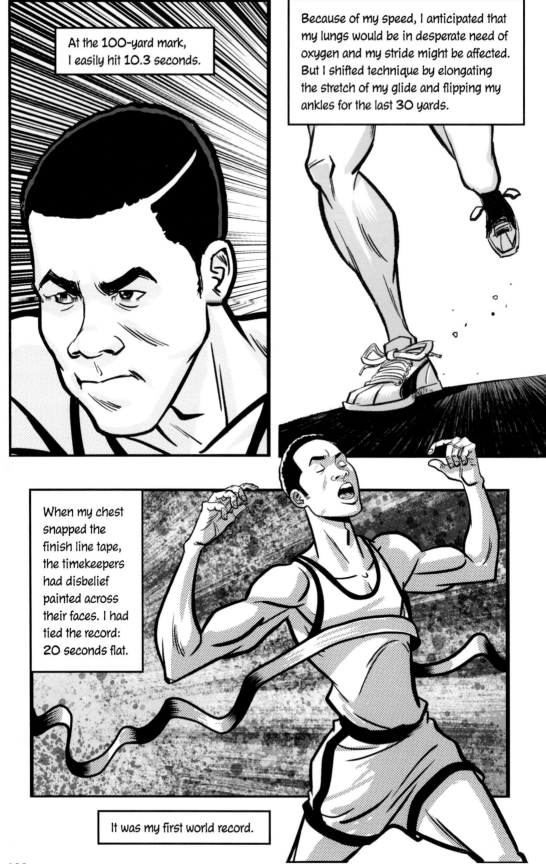

At the 100-yard mark, I easily hit 10.3 seconds.

Because of my speed, I anticipated that my lungs would be in desperate need of oxygen and my stride might be affected. But I shifted technique by elongating the stretch of my glide and flipping my ankles for the last 30 yards.

When my chest snapped the finish line tape, the timekeepers had disbelief painted across their faces. I had tied the record: 20 seconds flat.

It was my first world record.

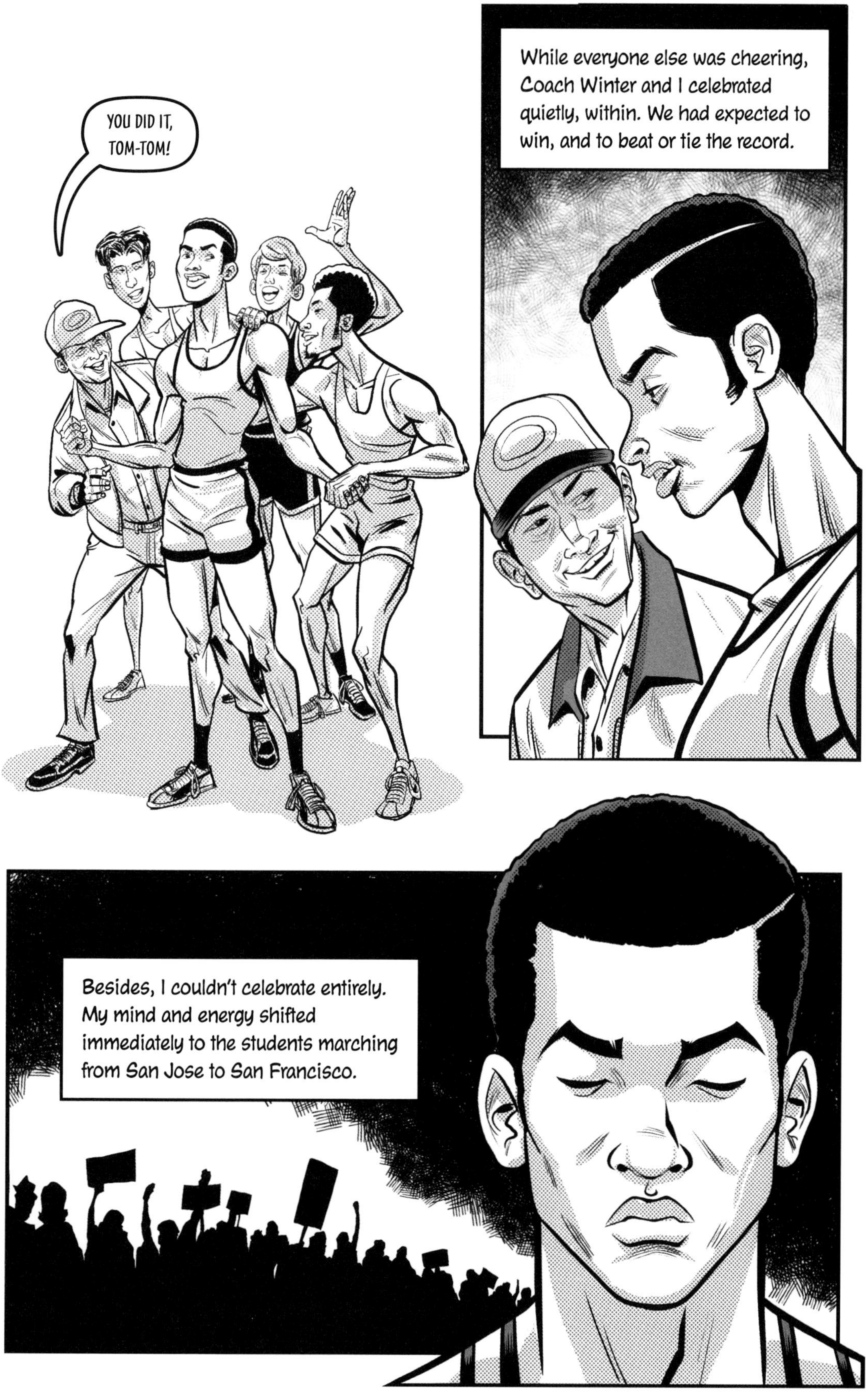
YOU DID IT, TOM-TOM!
While everyone else was cheering, Coach Winter and I celebrated quietly, within. We had expected to win, and to beat or tie the record.
Besides, I couldn't celebrate entirely. My mind and energy shifted immediately to the students marching from San Jose to San Francisco.

That evening, a friend drove me to a gymnasium in Sunnyvale. That's where the marchers were camped out for the night.

Many of them I didn't know. Most were Black, but there were some white students scattered across the crowded space.

I recognized and chatted up a few of the athletes I knew, and then found a space on the floor where I could lie down and rest for the night.

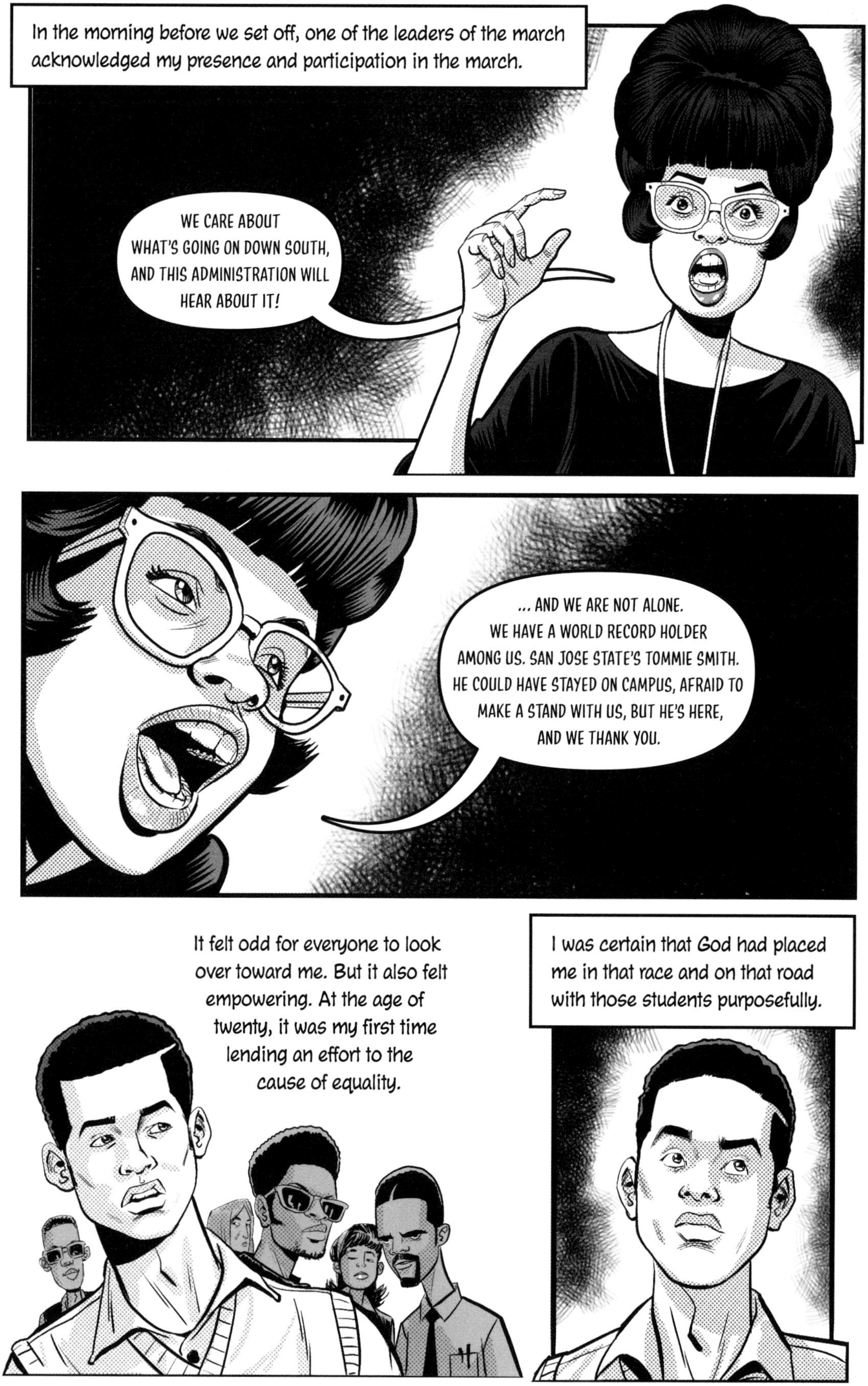
In the morning before we set off, one of the leaders of the march acknowledged my presence and participation in the march.
WE CARE ABOUT WHAT'S GOING ON DOWN SOUTH, AND THIS ADMINISTRATION WILL HEAR ABOUT IT!
... AND WE ARE NOT ALONE. WE HAVE A WORLD RECORD HOLDER AMONG US. SAN JOSE STATE'S TOMMIE SMITH. HE COULD HAVE STAYED ON CAMPUS, AFRAID TO MAKE A STAND WITH US, BUT HE'S HERE, AND WE THANK YOU.
It felt odd for everyone to look over toward me. But it also felt empowering. At the age of twenty, it was my first time lending an effort to the cause of equality.
I was certain that God had placed me in that race and on that road with those students purposefully.

On our way, we were harassed and yelled at by white motorists who streaked up and down the roadway waving their fists, screaming, and spitting from their car windows, even throwing bottles and cans.

At first I was frightened, then confused. What had we done to them? Hadn't they watched how those church folks were brutally beaten by those policemen in Alabama just six days prior?

I thought that perhaps they saw us as the problem. Maybe they saw us as troublemakers for just simply being . . .

. . . just simply being alive.

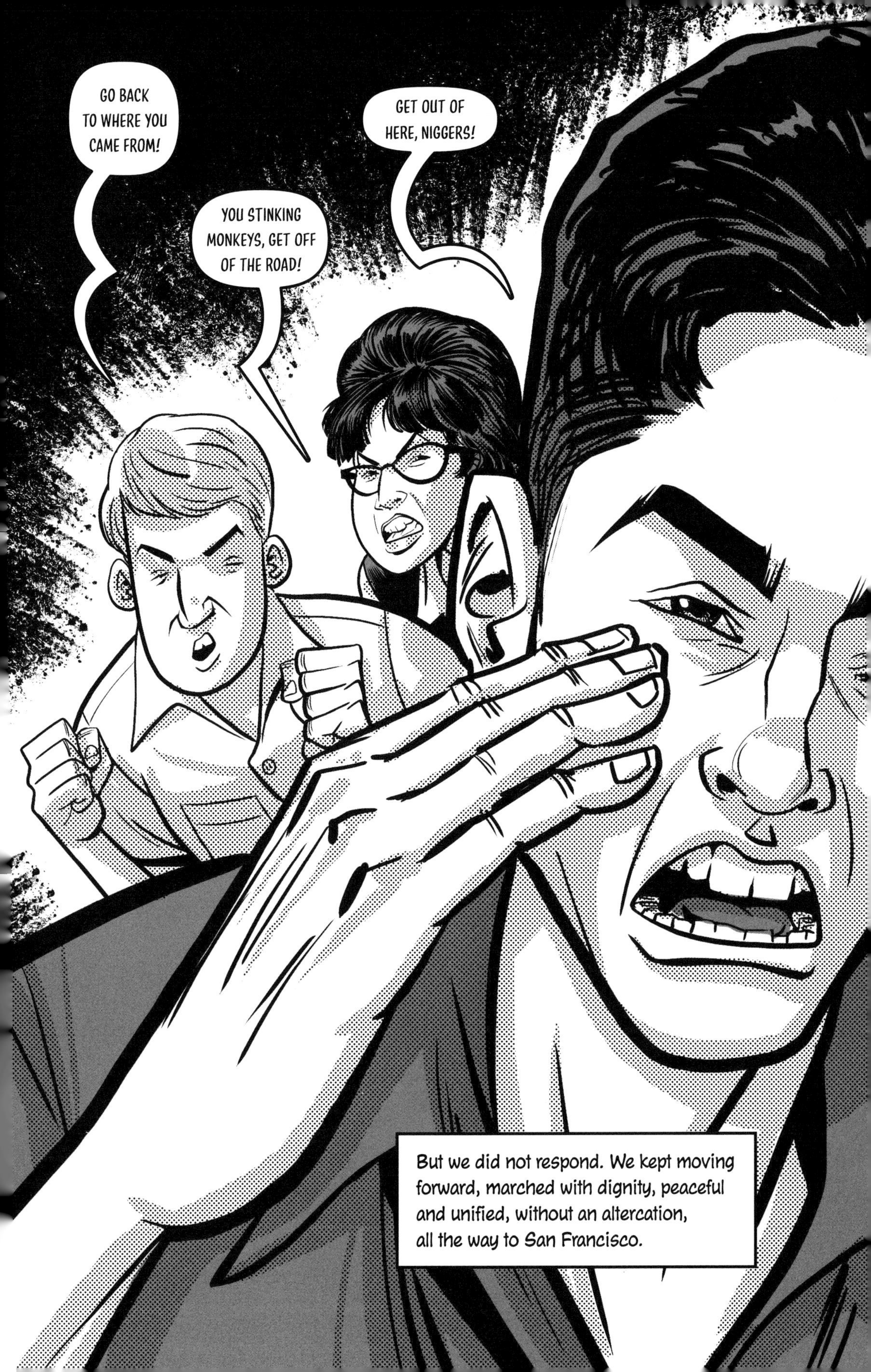
GO BACK TO WHERE YOU CAME FROM!
GET OUT OF HERE, NIGGERS!
YOU STINKING MONKEYS, GET OFF OF THE ROAD!
But we did not respond. We kept moving forward, marched with dignity, peaceful and unified, without an altercation, all the way to San Francisco.

The march drew a large crowd, and a few of us were interviewed. The local media knew that I was involved, and it felt empowering. It felt right.

It made me realize that I had an obligation—not just to carry the banner for San Jose State during track meets. I was obligated to carry an even larger banner for my people.

I would no longer remain silent, invisible. The world would soon know my name, most definitely on the track—and off.

I was also getting to know Harry Edwards.

You couldn't miss him. The brother was six foot eight, chest stuck out all the way to the Pacific, and brimming with confidence. Although he was built like an offensive tackle, he spoke and carried himself like a Rhodes scholar.

I learned a lot from him. His whole mind-set was on bettering not only the lives of Black folks across America but, particularly, the treatment of Black athletes.

He spoke frequently on how America uses the Black athlete for its gain, especially universities. He held court with all of the Black athletes on campus, making sure that we understood why we were there, and used our positions to advance the movement.

YOU CAN'T EAT RUNNING, SO DON'T LOOK AT WHATEVER SPORT YOU DO TO GET YOU THROUGH LIFE.

YOU'RE SMART ENOUGH TO KNOW YOU'RE RUNNING FAST, TOMMIE, SO USE IT.

He was big on Black men, Black people, taking ownership of our own bodies, our own lives.

1965
JANUARY

Twenty Black AFL football players chosen to play in the annual All-Star game arrive in New Orleans.

Cab drivers won't give them a lift . . .

Hotels refuse to welcome them . . .

They can't eat in the same restaurants or enter the same nightclubs as their white teammates.

Two Black players from the San Diego Chargers, Ernie Ladd and Earl Faison, call a meeting with the other Black players.

The men all vote not to play in the game as long as it remains in New Orleans. There would be no game without the Black players, so it is relocated and played the next day in Houston, Texas. It is the first time a professional sporting event in America is rescheduled as a result of Black athletes unifying to combat racial discrimination.

It was beautiful. It was powerful. It was a wake-up alarm for all of us.

Many great Black athletes during this time, like Muhammad Ali, who refused to join the armed forces and fight in Vietnam, in large part because of the continued hatred toward Black people . . .

Bill Russell, who fought racial prejudice and discrimination to become the first Black head coach in the NBA . . .

and young Lew Alcindor, who supported Ali's Vietnam War protest as the top collegiate basketball player in the country . . .

. . . were looked upon as beacons, bright defiant lights for the rest of young Black America to follow.

I was determined to be one of those men.

JUNIOR AND SENIOR YEARS, 1965–67

As a junior and a senior, I broke, set, and held multiple world records simultaneously:

MAY 1966
220y (straight): 19.5, San Jose

I was one of the fastest men on the planet—if not the fastest.

MAY 1966
220y (turn): 20.0, Sacramento

FEBRUARY 1967
440y: 46.2, Louisville

MAY 1967
4x220y relay: 01:22.1, Fresno

MAY 1967
400m: 44.5, San Jose

MAY 1967
440m: 44.8, San Jose

Sports Illustrated
BLAZING QUARTER-MILER
Tommie Smith of San Jose

In May 1967 I even made the cover of *Sports Illustrated*!

Coach Winter's wife promised to make any member of the track team an upside-down cake if they broke a record. I was the sole recipient. In fact, she owed me about six cakes.

But even with all those records, I was still one broke, and usually hungry, college student. We did so much for the school, but those actions were never reciprocated. It was time for us to make a statement, on campus and beyond.

In the late summer of 1967, with the 1968 Olympic Games in Mexico City approaching, Harry Edwards and a graduate student and long-distance athlete named Ken Noel called together as many Black collegiate athletes as they could to form the Olympic Project for Human Rights.

The founding statement of the OPHR addressed our impassioned ideals and goals:

We must no longer allow the sports world to pat itself on the back as a citadel of racial justice when the racial injustices of the sports industry are infamously legendary. Any black person who allows himself to be used in the above manner ... is a traitor to his country because he allows racist whites the luxury of resting assured that those black people in the ghettos are there because that is where they want to be.

So we ask, Why should we run in Mexico only to crawl home?

Star Black athletes from around the country were notified, including the track and field athletes from San Jose State—Speed City—who would make up the majority of the 1968 Olympic team.

I was front and center, and so was one of my good friends and teammates, Lee Evans.

Lee was from a farming family in central California, just like I was. We were both on the executive committee for the United Black Students for Action on campus. Lee was compact, raw, and strong, and a very fast sprinter. We competed hard, but always in good spirits.

And it was Lee who made me aware of another pivotal member of Speed City and the OPHR, a cocky, loquacious guy from Harlem, New York.

John Carlos.

John transferred from East Texas State University during my junior year. He specialized in the 100 meters and the 200 meters. He'd learned about Harry, Lee, and myself from a magazine article. Plus, he had experienced racism on the campus of East Texas and within his team.

His coach was a negative, mean, and belligerent type.

He had once swung a hammer at John. He had racist ideas about Black athletes, believing that we had non-human bone structure that gave us athletic advantages.

The opportunity to run with a team as fast as we were and to have a chance to be a part of challenging the system was too good to pass up.

I CAN'T TAKE THE HEAT HERE, MAN ... DON'T LIKE THE SNUBS ... THE RESTRICTED HOUSING ... THE WHOLE PHONY DEAL.

SO ... WHAT ARE YOU GOING TO DO?

He was meant to join us.

At the same time, we were letting our presence be known on our own campus.

There were issues that needed to be addressed, particularly the lack of housing. Black athletes stayed wherever they could because no one would rent to us.

I NOTICED THE VACANCY SIGN IN THE WINDOW, AND ...

NOPE. ALREADY TAKEN ... SORRY. GOOD DAY.

ROOM FOR RENT INQUIRE WITHIN

Saint Saffold and I were lucky enough to be helped out by the athletic department, but racist housing practices had most of us sleeping in garages, in barns, or on couches in the dorms.

Harry gave the administration at San Jose State a list of demands . . .
. . . more Black professors,
. . . more Black coaches,
. . . for San Jose State to do everything within its power to support the housing needs of its Black students on and off campus.

They laughed in his face.

We were not a priority. We, the children of sharecroppers and farm hands, and the grandchildren of slaves, had no right to make demands.

How dare we, ungrateful and disillusioned Negroes?

If our demands were not met, we said, we would hold a mighty, peaceful protest that would prevent the San Jose State football team from facing the University of Texas at El Paso, for the first game of the 1967 season.

The administration knew that we meant business. They were afraid of Harry's ties to the Black Panthers, a budding anti–police brutality group. The Panthers patrolled poor neighborhoods in West Oakland and provided services like free meals and tutoring, and made sure that the police did not abuse their authority.

The entire state became aware of the potential game stoppage, particularly the governor, Ronald Reagan.

CAN YOU IMAGINE ... STOPPING THE GAME? THE UNIVERSITY AND THE CITY SHOULD DO EVERYTHING THAT THEY CAN TO PUT AN END TO THAT PROTEST. THAT ... PROFESSOR, ... EDWARDS, IS NOT FIT TO TEACH. HE IS CONTRIBUTING NOTHING TOWARD HARMONY BETWEEN THE RACES.

RONALD REAGAN IS A PETRIFIED PIG, UNFIT TO GOVERN ...

To everyone's surprise, the game was canceled. We began to realize how much power we had to bring about righteousness, fairness, equality.

THE BLACK ATHLETE HAS LEFT THE FACADE OF LOCKER-ROOM EQUALITY AND JUSTICE TO TAKE HIS LONG-VACANT PLACE AS A PRIMARY PARTICIPANT IN THE BLACK REVOLUTION.

Now our sights were set on a larger stage, with international goals. The 1968 Summer Olympics.

I was active in the movement but not very vocal. That changed in September 1967.

I ran in Tokyo at the World University Games. I took home first place in the 200 meters.

After the meet I was crowded with microphones from seemingly every country in the world.

A Japanese reporter was the first to approach me with questions.

IN THE UNITED STATES, ARE THE NEGROES NOW EQUAL TO THE WHITES IN THE WAY THEY ARE TREATED?

NOT AT ALL.

WHAT ABOUT THE POSSIBILITY OF NEGROES BOYCOTTING THE 1968 OLYMPICS?

DEPENDING UPON THE SITUATION, YOU CANNOT RULE OUT THE POSSIBILITY THAT WE, THE NEGRO ATHLETES, MIGHT BOYCOTT THE OLYMPIC GAMES.

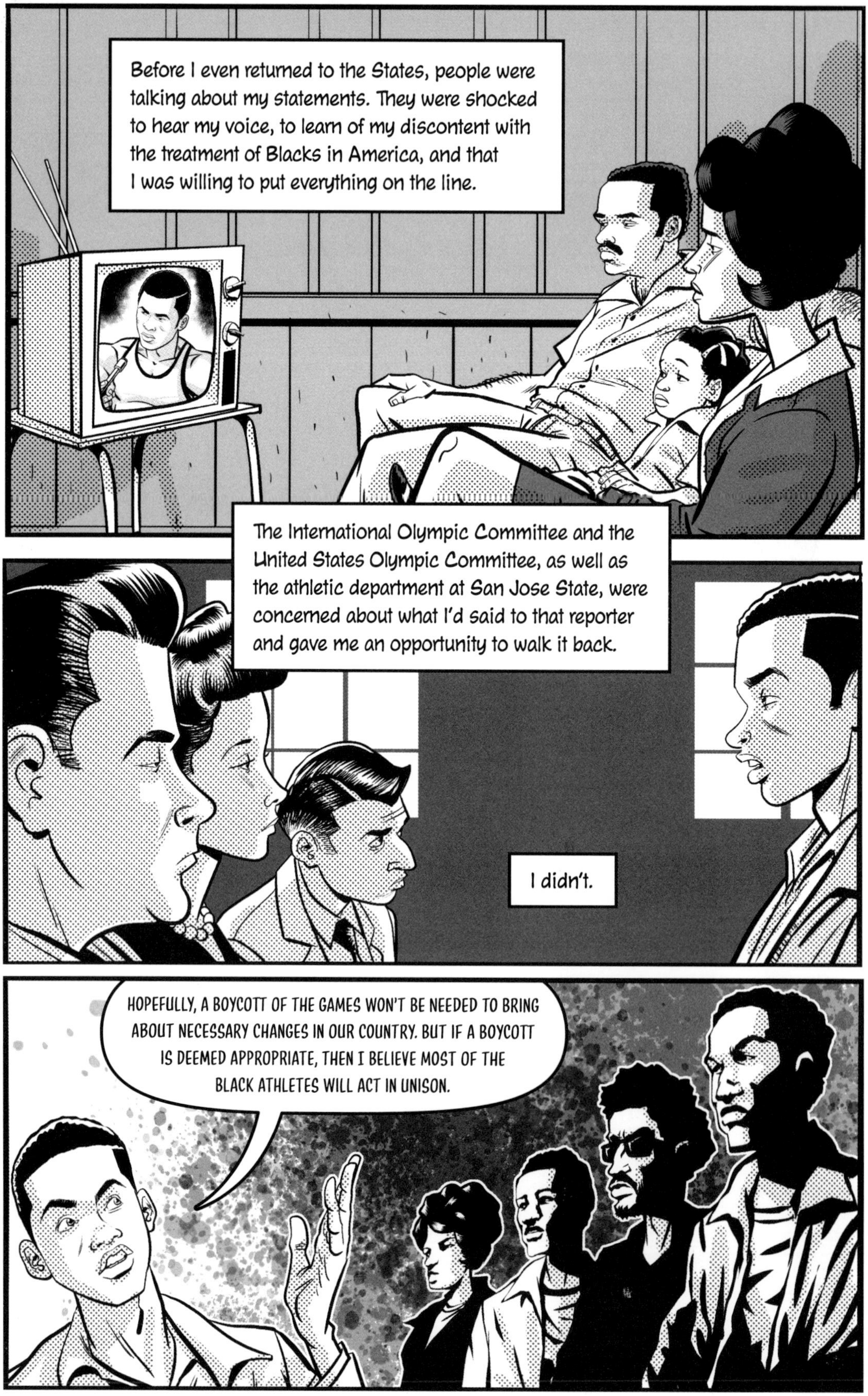
Before I even returned to the States, people were talking about my statements. They were shocked to hear my voice, to learn of my discontent with the treatment of Blacks in America, and that I was willing to put everything on the line.
The International Olympic Committee and the United States Olympic Committee, as well as the athletic department at San Jose State, were concerned about what I'd said to that reporter and gave me an opportunity to walk it back.
I didn't.
HOPEFULLY, A BOYCOTT OF THE GAMES WON'T BE NEEDED TO BRING ABOUT NECESSARY CHANGES IN OUR COUNTRY. BUT IF A BOYCOTT IS DEEMED APPROPRIATE, THEN I BELIEVE MOST OF THE BLACK ATHLETES WILL ACT IN UNISON.

A slew of hate mail called me ungrateful, uppity, unpatriotic, and every despicable thing beneath God's great sun.

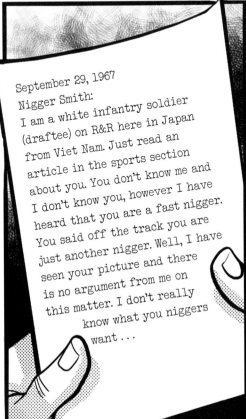

September 29, 1967

Nigger Smith:

I am a white infantry soldier (draftee) on R&R here in Japan from Viet Nam. Just read an article in the sports section about you. You don't know me and I don't know you, however I have heard that you are a fast nigger. You said off the track you are just another nigger. Well, I have seen your picture and there is no argument from me on this matter. I don't really know what you niggers want . . .

10/25/67

Dear Traitor,

You are not only a disgrace to your College, your Country . . . but to yourself!

Please don't try to win a place on the Olympic Team. I'd rather have our Country finish last, without you, than first with you.

149

Two months later, on Thanksgiving Day, the Western Regional Black Youth Conference was held at the Second Baptist Church in Los Angeles. Every Black athlete interested in supporting the OPHR was invited.

Lee, John, and I rode down in the back of Harry's pickup truck—and it was freezing! We drove at night because we were afraid that someone would try to harm us.

There were more than fifty big-name college athletes, like Lew Alcindor and Michael Warren of the UCLA Bruins, and members of the Black Panthers, such as Huey Newton. Harry led a workshop focused on the participation of Black athletes in the Olympics.

WHAT VALUE IS IT FOR A BLACK MAN TO WIN A GOLD MEDAL BUT RETURN TO THE HELL OF HARLEM?!

The demands of the OPHR were shared with everyone that day:

The hiring of more Black coaches on collegiate and professional sports teams.

That world heavyweight champion Muhammad Ali be reinstated and all charges against him be dropped.

That no team from South Africa be invited to the Summer Olympics. The country had been under systemic white-minority rule where segregation was a part of the law ever since 1948.

That Avery Brundage, a known bigot, and a man who had made public statements sympathetic toward Nazi Germany before the 1936 Summer Olympics, be removed from his position as the president of the International Olympic Committee.

Also present was Dr. Martin Luther King Jr. When he spoke, he was just as he was when I had seen him on television: reverent, captivating, powerful, sincere.

Huey Newton spoke, Harry spoke, even John stood before everyone to share his beliefs.

I sat in the back of the room and just listened. It had been a skill of mine ever since I was a boy.

The difference now, at the age of twenty-three and a rising senior, was that I had life experience. I was educated. I had come a long way, but on that day, among so many great orators and thinkers, even in my silence, I knew that I belonged.

1968

In February, hundreds gathered outside a track meet at Madison Square Garden, in New York, to protest the New York Athletic Club's practice of discriminating against people of color. Most of the Black athletes slated to participate pulled out, and the meet was a failure. We had made a huge statement. But there was a price to pay . . .

Athletes received death threats. Harry Edwards's apartment and car were vandalized, trashed with sewage and garbage. His pet dogs were killed and left in pieces for him to find.

Evil, pure evil for having the audacity to threaten an Olympic boycott.

Also in February, Lew Alcindor, the biggest college basketball star in the country, announced that he would not be trying out for the men's Olympic team.

APRIL 4

Our greatest champion of justice is brutally shot and killed on the balcony of a room at the Lorraine Motel in Memphis, Tennessee. He had been there to fight against the unfair treatment of Black sanitation workers.

"EVEN IN OUR SLEEP, PAIN WHICH CANNOT FORGET FALLS DROP BY DROP UPON THE HEART" ... FOR THOSE OF YOU WHO ARE BLACK AND ARE TEMPTED TO BE FILLED WITH HATRED AND MISTRUST OF THE INJUSTICE OF SUCH AN ACT, AGAINST ALL WHITE PEOPLE, I WOULD ONLY SAY THAT I CAN ALSO FEEL IN MY OWN HEART THE SAME KIND OF FEELING. I HAD A MEMBER OF MY FAMILY KILLED, BUT HE WAS KILLED BY A WHITE MAN.

In one of the poorest parts of Indianapolis, Indiana, presidential candidate Robert F. Kennedy stands in the back of a pickup truck and announces King's death to a massive crowd of Blacks. His brother President John F. Kennedy had been assassinated just four and a half years before.

Only two months later, on June 5, Robert Kennedy, on the campaign trail in a hotel in Los Angeles, is shot and killed. The country is a powder keg, set to explode at any moment, in any place.

At the end of June, the first Olympic trials were held in Los Angeles.

Many of the athletes who supported our movement wore Olympic Project for Human Rights buttons.

OLYMPIC PROJECT FOR HUMAN RIGHTS

Those who qualified moved onward to the final qualifying events, held in September in Echo Summit, California, where a track had been built near a mountain pass 7,382 feet above sea level. The goal was to simulate the high altitude we would contend with in Mexico City, a similar 7,350 feet above sea level.

The top three qualifiers in each event would represent the United States in October at the Games of the XIX Olympiad.

Among the athletes who made the team were some of the best in Olympic history:

Geoff Vanderstock (USC): 48.8 seconds in the 400-meter intermediate hurdles—new record.

John Carlos (Speed City): 19.7 seconds in the 200-meter sprint—new record (unfortunately nullified because he wasn't wearing the right spikes).

Lee Evans (Speed City): 44.06 seconds in the 400-meter sprint—new record.

Bob Beamon (UTEP): 27 feet, 6.5 inches in the long jump.

Bob Seagren (SoCal Striders): 17 feet, 9 inches in the pole vault.

Tommie Smith (Speed City).

157

Surprisingly, as the start of the games approached, a couple of the OPHR's demands were met! Black coaches and officials were added to the teams. South Africa was banned from the games.

Although a complete boycott would have sent an undeniably strong message, we Black athletes decided to compete. We would all decide, on our own, how we would protest the state of race relations in America. None of us knew what any of us would do, if anything at all.

I DON'T THINK ANY OF THESE BOYS WILL BE FOOLISH ENOUGH TO DEMONSTRATE AT THE OLYMPIC GAMES ...

I THINK IF THEY DO, THEY'LL BE PROMPTLY SENT HOME ...

Avery Brundage, the International Olympic Committee president, knew of our intent to compete and still make various statements against injustice. He showed zero understanding of the plight of Black Americans. To him, the Olympics would not be a stage for our activism.

For white Americans who had no interest in the plight or advancement of Black people, we were still viewed as the problem. I was on the cover of *Newsweek* magazine, with the headline "THE ANGRY BLACK ATHLETE."

The leader and most visible mouthpiece for the OPHR movement, Harry Edwards, was advised to not attend the games. He had been tracked by federal agents and sent constant death threats.

But we were not alone. We had each other's backs. For Black people across America, it had always been that way.

Ten days before the start of the Olympic games, the Mexican army purposefully aimed and fired on thousands of students protesting in Mexico City for a better future for their homeland.

The government stomped out the protest and even cleaned up—washed away its own evil actions by painting over the bloody pavement. To visitors to the city, arriving from all over the world, it was as if nothing had ever taken place . . .

The games went on without many of the 5,516 athletes representing over 112 countries ever knowing.

This would be the first time in Olympic history that the games would be held in a Spanish-speaking country . . .

. . . and the first time that a woman would start off the events by running with the torch and lighting the ceremonial cauldron's eternal flame.

That honor went to Mexican hurdler Enriqueta Basilio.

I had a feeling as I walked around the stadium in my ceremonial first-day outfit—fancy hat, slacks, and a nice suit jacket—that more "firsts" were bound to happen.

Ciudad Universitaria, Mexico
Estadio Olímpico Universitario

The fourth day of the games . . .
It was time for our event, the 200 meters.
John easily won his first heat in 20.5
seconds. I set an Olympic record in
the second heat with a time of 20.37

Quarter-finals: John came in first again (20.69),
and so did the speedy Australian Peter Norman (20.44),
who was showing that he would be someone for the both of us
to deal with in the finals.

In the third quarter,
just thirty minutes after
my last race,
I one-upped myself by
setting a new record:
20.28.

The semifinals were set up to be super competitive. John and Peter Norman were in the same race. And just like that, John obliterated my newly minted record with a 20.12. Peter didn't do too bad, either, finishing in 20.22 seconds.

My semifinal was next. I didn't have any worries about finishing first, but my time would determine my lane in the final. And way in the back of my mind, I had an irrational fear that someone, some crazy person, would attempt to shoot and kill one of us, in mid-race.

I couldn't dwell on that idea for long or it would affect my race, and even though there was some surface worry, I was not made to fear man. There was an armor around me, a mental and spiritual armor.

So I bowed my head, as I always did before a race, and said a short prayer.

163

I exploded out of the blocks cleanly, made a textbook turn, and was soon gliding toward the straightaway for my third victory.

AND HE'S REALLY POWERING IT AWAY! THE 'TOMMIE JET' THEY CALL HIM!

BANG!

First place, in 20.14. But as I crossed the finish line, it felt as if a sniper high up in the stands had been able to get a clear shot. One of the wackos who had sent hateful death-threat letters had come through on his promise to keep me from ever winning Olympic gold.

When I looked down, I was shocked to discover that there was no blood.

My adductor muscle in my left thigh was severely pulled. I couldn't even walk.

The pain was excruciating, and if there was one thought, other than the fear of assassination, it was that I might not be able to run in the finals.

COME ON, TOM-TOM. WE'LL GET YOU TAKEN CARE OF.

I fell to the ground and closed my eyes. When I opened them and looked up, there were faint sunbeams balancing over the shoulder of a smiling Coach Winter.

The trainers and Coach Winter did an ice-on and ice-off method for about forty-five minutes, which put an end to the swelling.

I'M GONNA BE HERE FOR A WHILE ... MAYBE EVEN FOREVER.

Coach walked me out to the training field. Forty minutes remained before the finals. I walked up a set of steps, very slowly, to see if I could exert any force on my groin area.

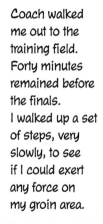

It was a success.

LOOKING GOOD, TOMMIE. LET'S GET A GOOD JOG GOING.

I gave my leg a good 60% during the jog. It felt good, yet time was ticking and the sun had begun to wane.

Out there on that practice field, I thought of everything I had gone through to get there. All of my early days in Texas. Mulla and my father and how much they had sacrificed for me.

I thought of every one of my siblings. I thought about being out in those fields in California until the moonlight covered us completely. I thought of my newlywed wife, Denise, and our baby son, Kevin. I had come a long way, and there was no way I would miss this race. My will to compete and the positive energy that surged through my body gave me the certainty that it was time.

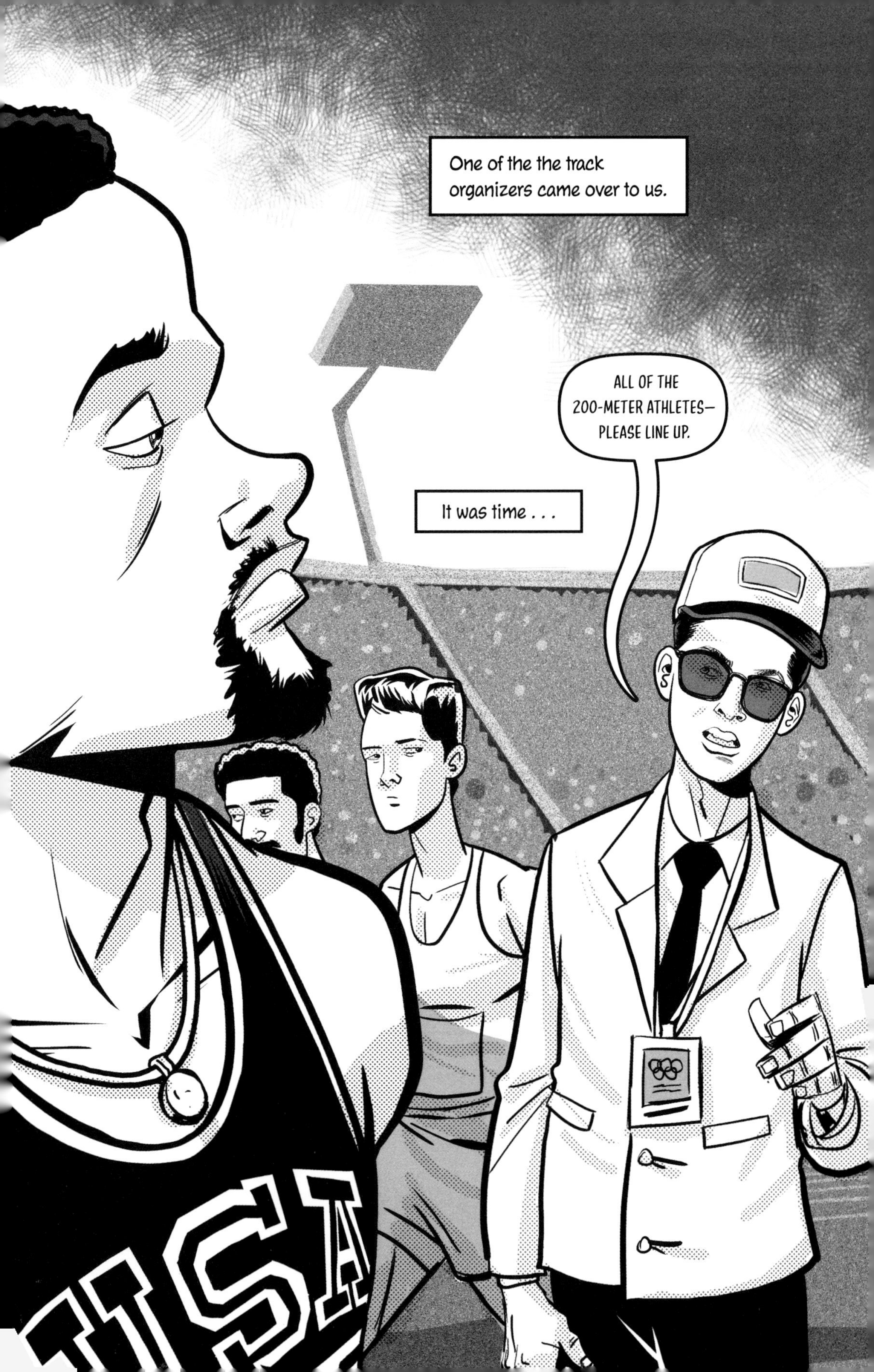

One of the the track organizers came over to us.
ALL OF THE 200-METER ATHLETES— PLEASE LINE UP.
It was time . . .
USA

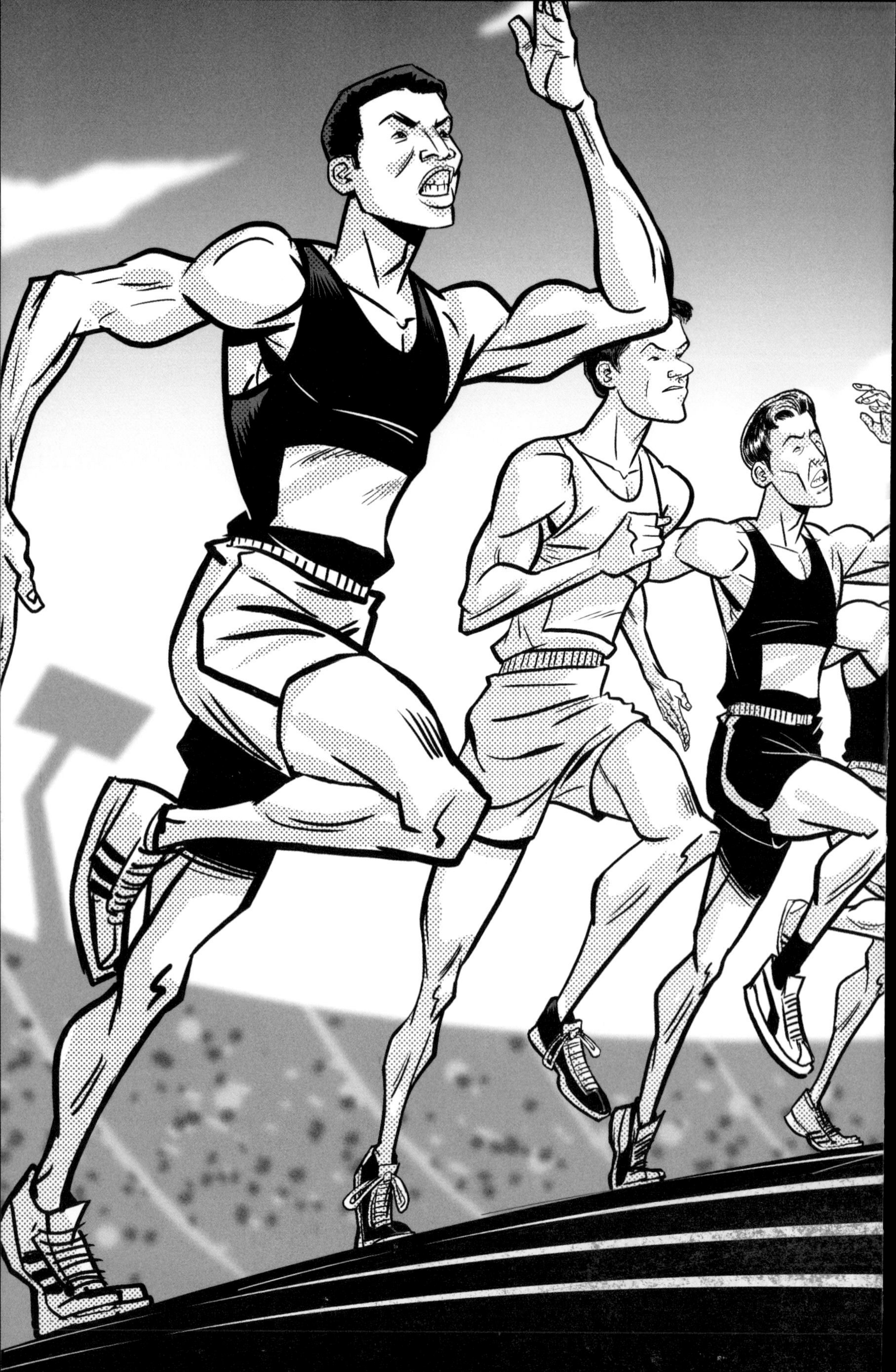

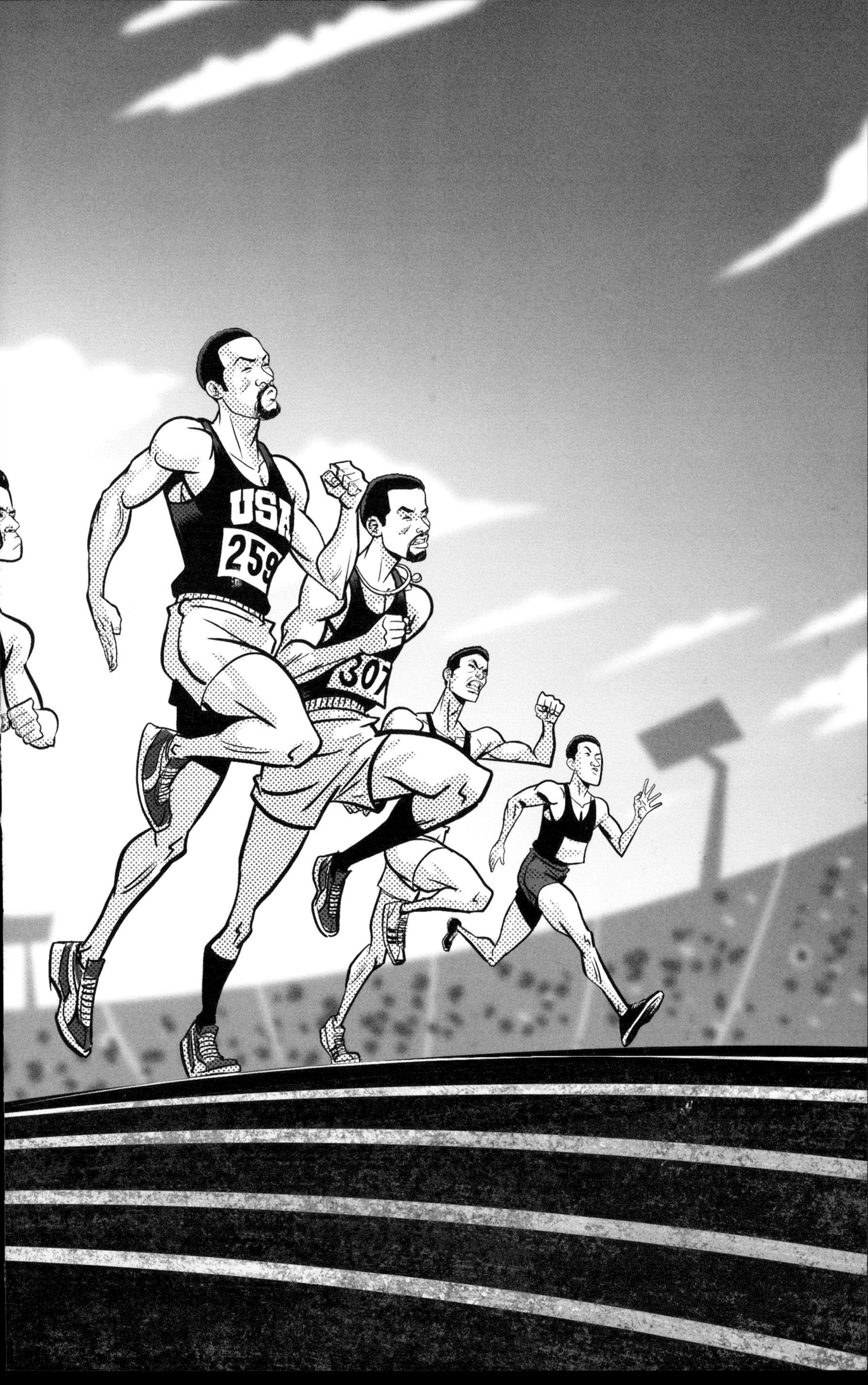
USA
259
307

John maintained the lead all the way around the turn. When we hit the straightaway, I put on the jets.

I was not accustomed to following behind runners. I was the pacesetter. This was my time to press the gas.

I was within ten feet of him when he made the mistake of looking back. In that one stride I passed him. If there were ever flames roaring from my feet, it was that day. Those last 80 meters were a blur, a glorious record-breaking blur.

I raised my hands to the sky as I crossed the finish line:

19.83 seconds. Another world record! At the age of twenty-four, I became the first man to run the 200-meter race in under 20 seconds.

Peter Norman took second place, the silver medal, and my teammate John Carlos took the bronze.

John draped an arm across my shoulders. We congratulated each other like brothers.

But we knew that the time had come.

Nothing was planned specifically. We'd had brief talks. We decided that we would follow each other's lead, and at the same time express ourselves the way we wanted to, as individuals.

I guess you could call it "planned spontaneity." When the time came, we would know what to do.

We both took off our Pumas to expose our black socks, which represented the impoverished children and families around the world and in every major city and crowded ghetto in America.

John unzipped his jacket, which went against Olympic rules, to represent the hardworking, blue-collar folks in America who struggle to make ends meet.

He also wore a beaded necklace, and I wore a black scarf. With those two items, we were representing the innumerable Black men in America who had been lynched.

Our wives, Denise and Kim, had bought a pair of black leather gloves earlier in the day . . .

We both had on an Olympic Project for Human Rights button.

WOULD YOU LIKE A BUTTON TO WEAR OUT THERE?

I'D LOVE TO SUPPORT, MATE.

I APPRECIATE THAT.

Peter got an extra button from a kid on the row team named Paul Hoffman.

John and I stood there, patiently, clutching our sneakers in our hands behind our backs, with our spirits humbled and our heads bowed.

Every chance I got, I'd say a small prayer. There was no time better than that moment. If your soul wasn't right, you probably couldn't see it, couldn't feel it.

All of a sudden, I was aware of everything, but afraid of nothing.

They called our names one at a time—

GOLD MEDALIST— TEAM USA— TOMMIE SMITH!

I leaped on top of the highest platform of that victory stand, with the number one placard in front of it, and lifted both of my hands toward the heavens.

An official in a cherry-red blazer slid the gold medal with the green ribbon around my neck.

From the cotton fields of Texas and California . . .

. . . to an Olympic field in Mexico . . .

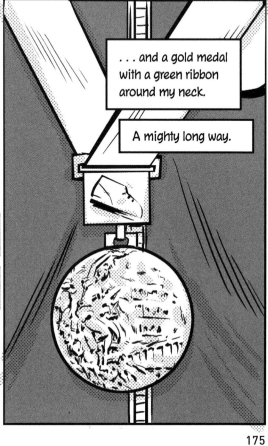

. . . and a gold medal with a green ribbon around my neck.

A mighty long way.

It was time.

First there was silence . . .

. . . and then the United States' national anthem began to blare across the stadium, over our heads, over the stands.

I clenched that fist with the black glove so tight, I could feel my knuckles pop and the tips of my nails pierce my palm.

John and I shared the pair of black leather gloves. He wore the left one, and I had on the right.

I held it up like a torch, defiant. There was no way I would place my hand over my heart and honor a flag for a country that did not honor me or people who looked like me.

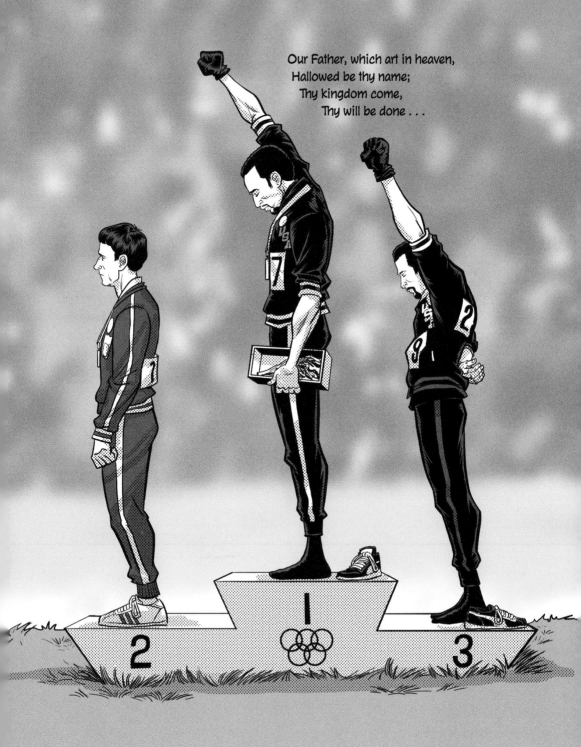

I could hear the wind whip around my forearm. My eyes were closed as the anthem went on in the background of my mind. I bowed my head again, I talked to God—

Our Father, which art in heaven,
Hallowed be thy name;
Thy kingdom come,
Thy will be done . . .

Eighty seconds.
That's how long we stood
there as the anthem played.

Those fists in the air were
dedicated to everyone at home,
back in the projects in Chicago,
Oakland, and Detroit,
to everyone in the boroughs
of Queens and Brooklyn,
to all of the brothers
and sisters, fathers and mothers
in Birmingham, Atlanta, Dallas,
Houston, St. Louis, New Orleans,
to everyone struggling, working
their fingers to the bone
on farms across America,
to everyone holding out hope
that things will get better . . .

. . . that was for you,
from John and me.

We had to be seen because
we were not being heard.

CHAPTER 4

STILL STANDING TALL

When we stepped off the stand and walked off the track, we heard cheers mixed with jeers and booing. I lifted my fist again, in anger.

Harry Edwards had once called International Olympic Committee president Avery Brundage "our Bull Connor," after the racist politician from Alabama who did everything in his power to fight against equality for Black people.

I HAD SAID THAT IF THERE WERE ANY DEMONSTRATIONS AT THE OLYMPIC GAMES, BY ANYONE, THE PARTICIPANTS WOULD BE SENT HOME!

We were suspended by the U.S. Olympic Committee and given only forty-eight hours to pack our things, leave the Olympic Village, and board a plane back to the States. I did not run in the 400m and John did not run in the 100m.

Our Olympic careers, right then and there, came to a screeching halt.

Before we left, John and I were interviewed by a British reporter.

DO YOU THINK THE OLYMPIC GAMES IS THE RIGHT PLACE TO DO THIS SORT OF THING? THAT YOU OUGHT TO USE THIS AS A WORLD STAGE?

WE USED THIS SO THAT THE WHOLE WORLD COULD SEE THE POVERTY OF THE BLACK MAN IN AMERICA.

AT THE SAME TIME, CYNICS MAY SAY THAT YOU HAVE IT ALL. YOU HAVE THE MEDALS, PUBLICITY, YOU'VE GOT MARTYRDOM AS WELL. WHAT DO YOU SAY TO THAT?

I CAN'T EAT THAT, AND THE KIDS THAT GREW UP AROUND MY BLOCK CAN'T EAT THAT ... ALL WE ASK FOR IS AN EQUAL CHANCE, TO BE A HUMAN BEING ... AS FAR AS I SEE NOW, WE'RE FIVE STEPS BELOW THE LADDER, AND EVERY TIME WE TRY TO TOUCH THE LADDER, THEY PUT THEIR FEET ON OUR HANDS, AND DON'T WANT US TO CLIMB UP... .

Back home, American journalists called us "militants!"—as if fighting for the rights of our people was something to be ashamed of.

"...a couple of black-skinned storm troopers."

"...a juvenile gesture by a couple of athletes who should have known better."

"...An embarrassment ...an insult to their countrymen," wrote the *Chicago Tribune*.

"...A Nazi-like salute," wrote the *Los Angeles Times*.

I was fired from my job at North American Pontiac before we even left Mexico City.

PONTIAC

We were not welcomed with pride and open arms when we returned to San Jose State. The only exception was the college's president, Dr. Robert Clark, who had also supported our efforts for fair off-campus housing.

ALL AMERICANS SHOULD BE PROUD OF THEIR ACHIEVEMENTS ... I REGRET THAT OUR TREATMENT OF OUR BLACK ATHLETES HAS BEEN SUCH AS TO PROMPT THEM TO FEEL THEY MUST USE THE OLYMPIC GAMES TO COMMUNICATE THEIR REAL CONCERN FOR BLACKS IN AMERICA.

But many staff members and college alumni were not cut from the same cloth as Dr. Clark. They threatened to withdraw their financial support from the school. He ended up resigning the following year.

I did whatever I could to feed my wife and son: swept streets, washed cars, you name it. I held eleven track and field world records, but no one would hire me.

When I went back to my studies for senior year, I took night classes. I didn't want to be a target.

During my last semester, I returned to Lemoore to teach. It was a requirement for my degree.

Many of the folks who'd been there when I was a boy were still there. No one asked about the Olympics. They just thought that I was there to clean and buff the floors, the way I used to do during the summers with my father. But I was back as an educated man, a gold-medal-winning educated man.

When I graduated, in the spring of 1969, there was no teaching job waiting for me. My old roommate, Saint Saffold, was playing football for the Cincinnati Bengals and vouched for me with the owner of the team.

I signed with them, but I was primarily a practice squad player. In three years, I suited up for only two regular season games, catching one pass. It was a deep one, for forty-one yards.

Football wasn't my passion. I wanted to run again . . .

. . . but the USOC made sure that I couldn't compete, internationally or nationally.

I would have liked to have run in the 1972 Summer Olympics in Munich. I would have liked to continue to grow and mature as a runner, just to see how much faster I could have gotten.

God only knows. It never happened.

In 1970, my marriage to Denise ended. Just a few weeks later I received some news that I was not ready for. It crushed me . . .

TOMMIE ... ARE YOU AWAKE?

IT'S AFTER TWO A.M. IS EVERYTHING OKAY?

IT'S MULLA ... SHE WAS AT A CHURCH IN RIVERDALE, LISTENING TO GLADYS AND THE GIRLS SING ... SHE JUST ... SLUMPED OVER, TOMMIE. SHE'S GONE ...

It was a brain embolism, but I knew that in addition, she had probably died of heartbreak from receiving the same hateful mail I had, and seeing negative news stories about me.

My soul just couldn't take it, losing Mulla, my mother—dear sweet Dora Smith.

It felt like everything I loved was vanishing from my life.

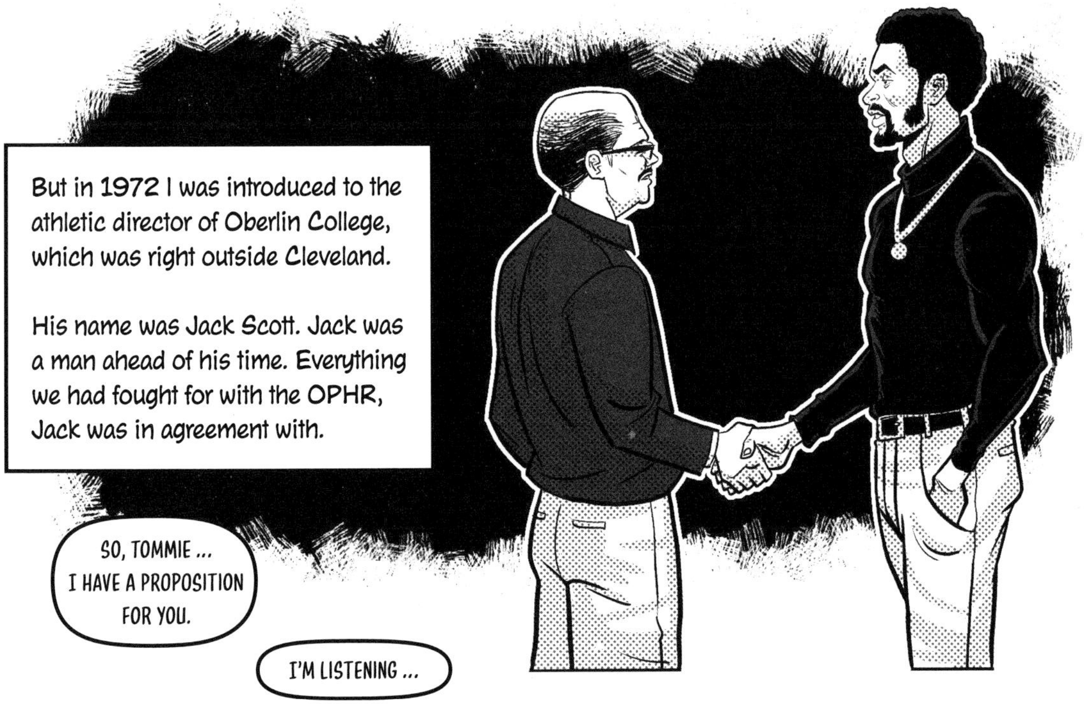
But in 1972 I was introduced to the athletic director of Oberlin College, which was right outside Cleveland.
His name was Jack Scott. Jack was a man ahead of his time. Everything we had fought for with the OPHR, Jack was in agreement with.
SO, TOMMIE ... I HAVE A PROPOSITION FOR YOU.
I'M LISTENING ...

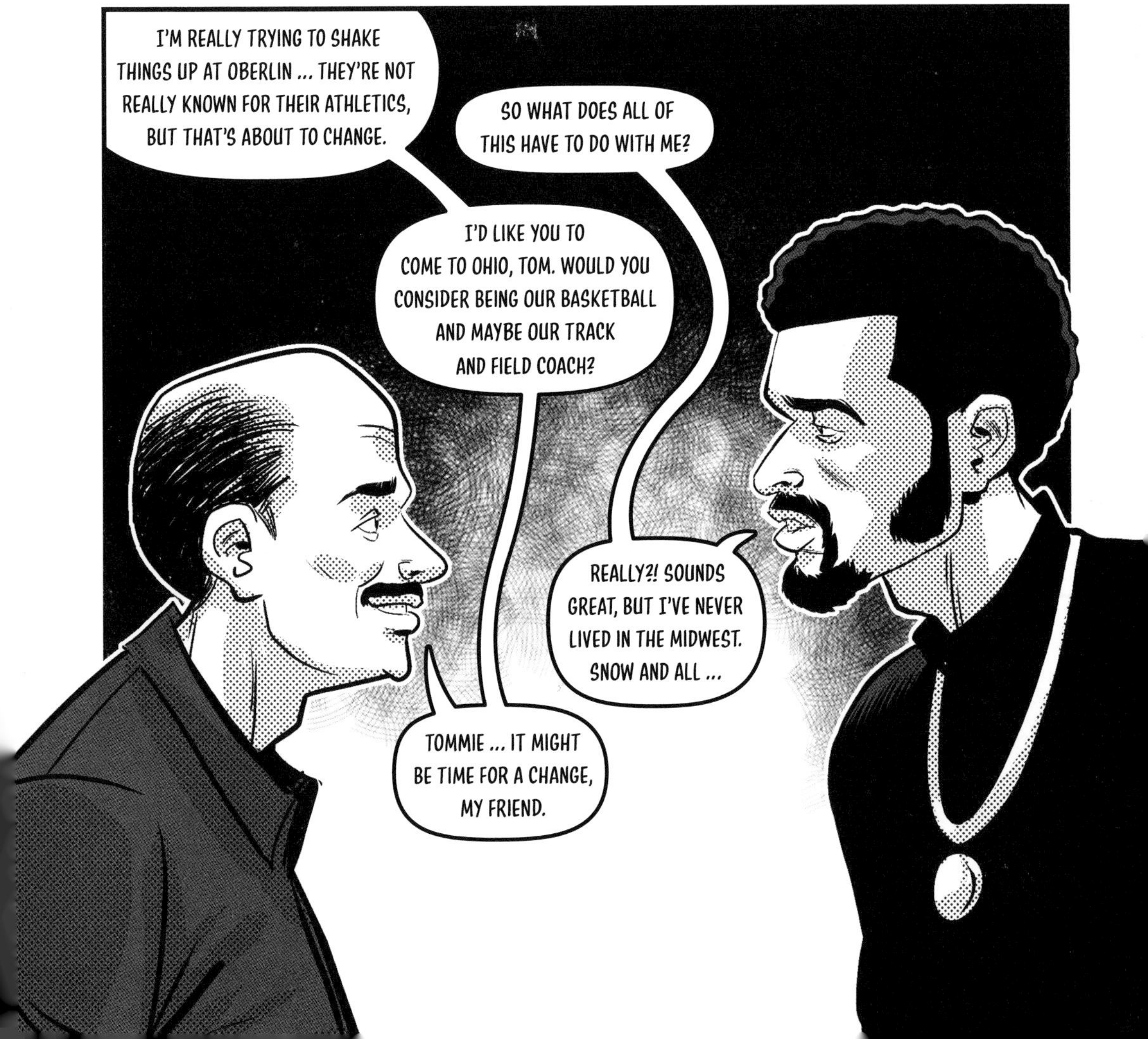
I'M REALLY TRYING TO SHAKE THINGS UP AT OBERLIN ... THEY'RE NOT REALLY KNOWN FOR THEIR ATHLETICS, BUT THAT'S ABOUT TO CHANGE.
SO WHAT DOES ALL OF THIS HAVE TO DO WITH ME?
I'D LIKE YOU TO COME TO OHIO, TOM. WOULD YOU CONSIDER BEING OUR BASKETBALL AND MAYBE OUR TRACK AND FIELD COACH?
REALLY?! SOUNDS GREAT, BUT I'VE NEVER LIVED IN THE MIDWEST. SNOW AND ALL ...
TOMMIE ... IT MIGHT BE TIME FOR A CHANGE, MY FRIEND.

It was the blessing I needed. The job paid me $14,000 to begin. I loaded up my car and drove to Ohio. It seemed so fitting, moving to Oberlin.

It was the first college in America to admit Black students and the first to admit women. It was also one of the stops for slaves escaping from the South.

I was ready for a change, but what I wasn't ready for was the Ohio winters. Part of the job was shoveling off the track for my kids, all by myself.

I was able to save enough money to pay for a master's degree program at Cambridge College in Massachusetts. I did most of my classwork over the phone, through the mail, and I even flew back and forth between Oberlin, Ohio, and Cambridge from time to time.

I took me three years to earn that degree. When I received the diploma, I displayed it high and prominently. It was a marker for how far I had still come and how much more I could accomplish.

I became the assistant athletic director, and my son, Kevin, came to live with me. In 1976 I got remarried, to a brilliant woman named Denise (like my first wife). I'd met her while teaching at Oberlin.

Unfortunately, I was let go from Oberlin College in 1978, so we packed up our things and moved back to California.

I was hired as the track and field coach at Santa Monica College. I held that position for twenty-seven years. While there, I sent countless track and field stars off to become champions and Olympic athletes.

Many also became track coaches themselves and came back to thank me for teaching them what I knew, for being so hard on them, for caring about their education and their lives . . .

. . . everything I'd learned from the great Bud Winter from my time at San Jose.

Denise and I had four children: Danielle, Timothy, Anthony Kyle, and Joey. We separated in 1997, and eventually divorced.

While I was living in an apartment in a bad neighborhood, many of my track and football memorabilia were stolen.

In 1998, I met a young woman named Delois in the administration office at Santa Monica College. She had no idea who I was or any of the baggage I carried with me.

We hit it off immediately. She was ALLLLL business. After we started dating, she began to negotiate marketing deals and speaking engagements for me.

But what really won me over was that she got on the phone to those organizations that had given me the rings and plaques that had been stolen from that apartment, and was able to have new ones sent to me. I knew then that she was the one.

She'd always look out for me, and I'd do anything and everything to look out for her.

We married in 2000.

She brought me peace.

Somewhere around that period, or maybe a few years before, things began to shift. I no longer felt like a pariah. The death threats dwindled, as did the sneers, the isolation, the darkness.

Organizations, universities, and schools across the country began to request that I come to speak about everything that had happened in my life—

people and places that would have never wanted to hear from me thirty years before. All of a sudden, everyone wanted to interview both John Carlos and me.

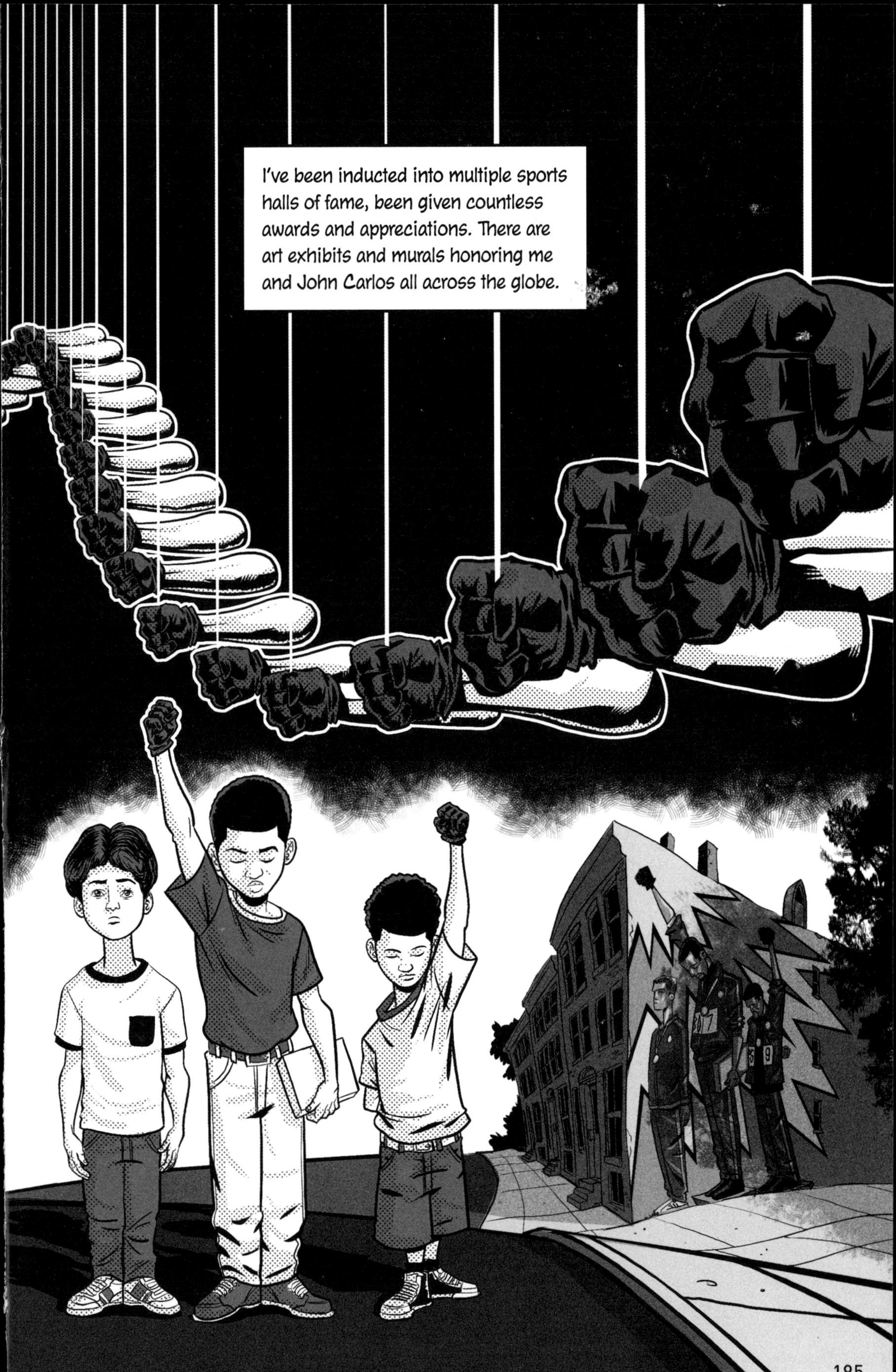
I've been inducted into multiple sports halls of fame, been given countless awards and appreciations. There are art exhibits and murals honoring me and John Carlos all across the globe.
17
9

In 2005, San Jose State had a twenty-two-foot-tall sculpture of John and me installed on the campus.

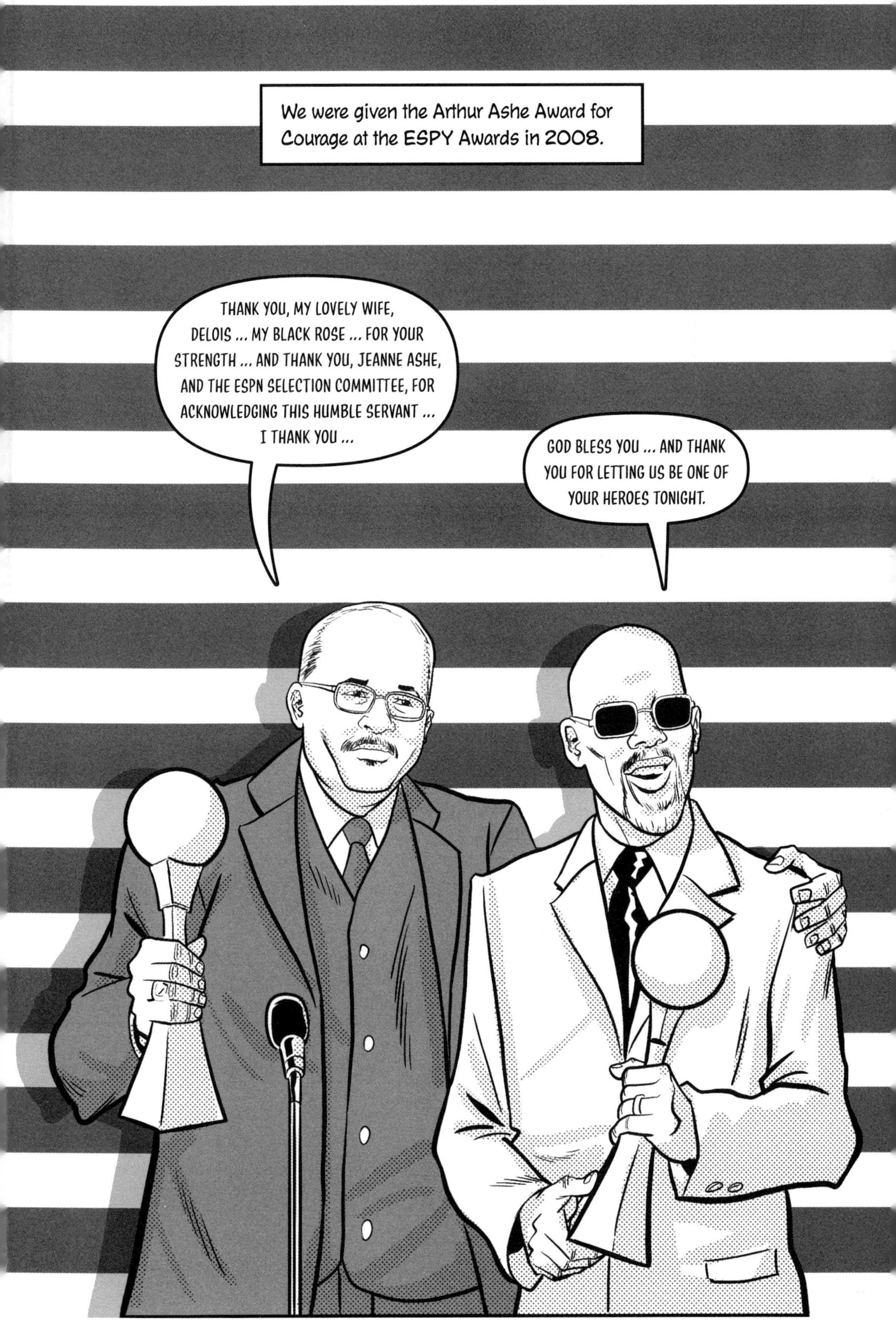
We were given the Arthur Ashe Award for Courage at the ESPY Awards in 2008.
THANK YOU, MY LOVELY WIFE, DELOIS ... MY BLACK ROSE ... FOR YOUR STRENGTH ... AND THANK YOU, JEANNE ASHE, AND THE ESPN SELECTION COMMITTEE, FOR ACKNOWLEDGING THIS HUMBLE SERVANT ... I THANK YOU ...
GOD BLESS YOU ... AND THANK YOU FOR LETTING US BE ONE OF YOUR HEROES TONIGHT.

In 2016, John and I were invited to the White House by the forty-fourth president of the United States, the first Black president in the history of the country, Barack Obama.

On November 1, 2019, at a ceremony in Colorado Springs, John and I were finally inducted into the U.S. Olympic and Paralympic Hall of Fame.

U.S. PARALYMPICS

U.S OLYMPIC & PARALYMPICS
HALL OF FAME

IT TAKES WORK FOR THINGS TO HAPPEN. IT TAKES TIME. BUT USUALLY, NOT FIFTY-ONE YEARS. BUT I'LL TAKE IT NOW AND ACCEPT IT FOR THE YOUNG MAN BACK IN 1968.

LONG OVERDUE ...

Now people call us heroes . . .
They say we were brave, courageous . . .
They say we served as a mountainous
source of inspiration . . .

CRAIG HODGES

MAHMOUD ABDUL-RAUF

LeBRON JAMES

THE ST. LOUIS RAMS
PLAYERS WHO PROTESTED THE MURDER OF MICHAEL BROWN

ERIC REID

COLIN KAEPERNICK

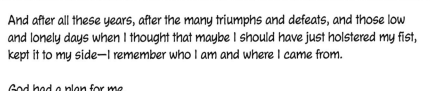

And after all these years, after the many triumphs and defeats, and those low and lonely days when I thought that maybe I should have just holstered my fist, kept it to my side—I remember who I am and where I came from.

God had a plan for me.

I hold no regrets. And if I could run that race again, blazing around that track, wind at my back and nothing but space in front of me, lifting my arms to the heavens as I burst through that finish line, I wouldn't hesitate, not one second . . .

if I could hoist that fist up to the heavens one more time . . .

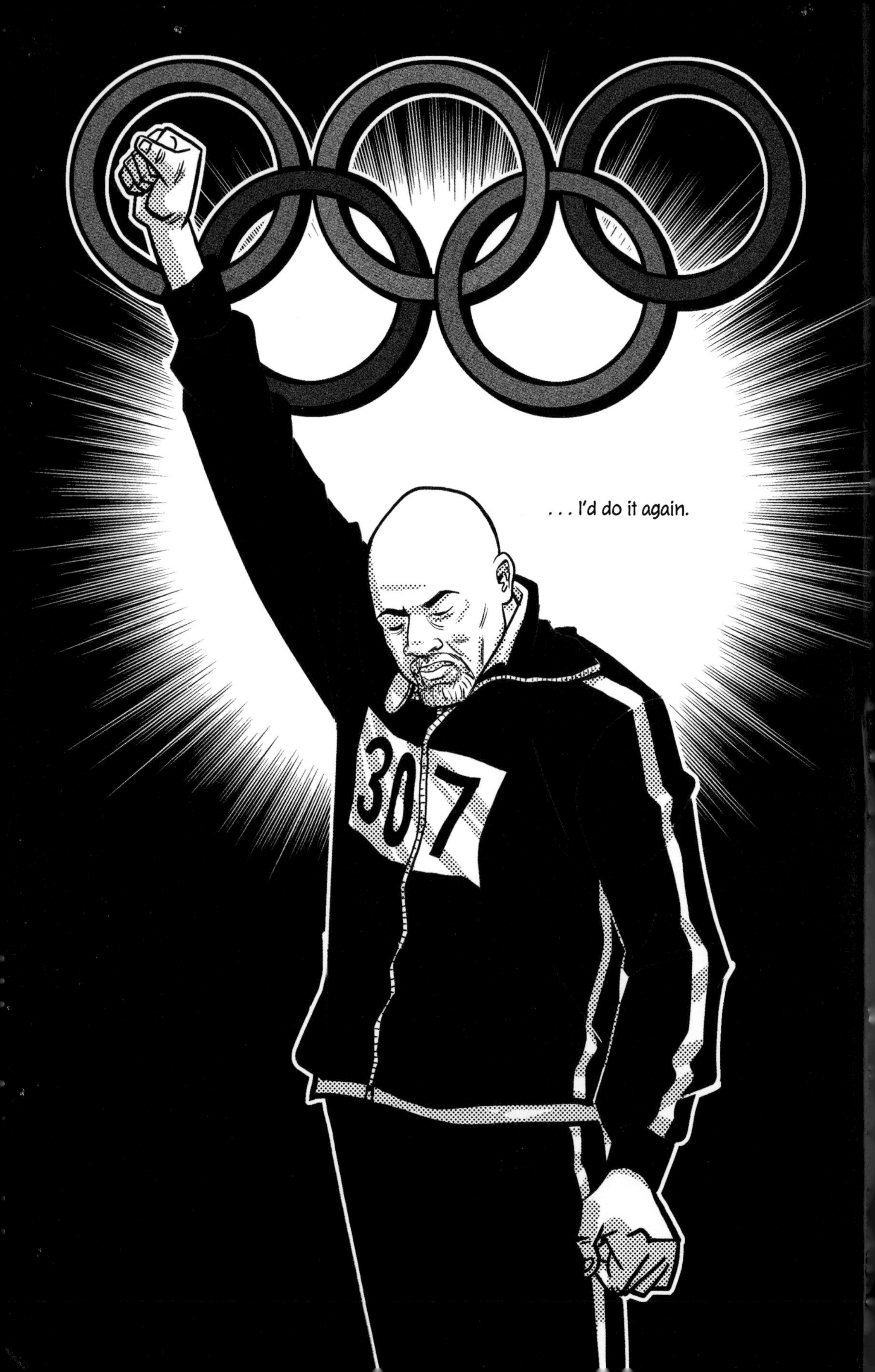

. . . I'd do it again.
307

ABOUT THE AUTHORS

DR. TOMMIE SMITH

was born near Clarksville, Texas, in 1944 and moved to California at the age of seven. An outstanding high school athlete, he earned a scholarship to San Jose State College, where he was a member of the "Speed City" track team that produced several noted Olympic athletes. He held as many as eleven world records simultaneously, and at the 1968 Olympic Games in Mexico City became the first man to officially run the 200 meters in under 20 seconds, setting a world record and winning the gold medal. His protest on the podium led to his removal from the Olympics, exclusion from subsequent national and world athletic competitions, death threats, and economic hardship. He went on to earn degrees in sociology and social change and was a teacher and coach at Oberlin College and Santa Monica College. Dr. Smith has received many awards and accolades, including the Arthur Ashe Award for Courage and the Courage of Conscience Award from the Peace Abbey Foundation for his lifelong commitment to athletics, education, and human rights.

DERRICK BARNES

is the author of the *New York Times* bestseller *The King of Kindergarten*, as well as the critically acclaimed picture book *Crown: An Ode to the Fresh Cut*, which received a Newbery Honor, a Coretta Scott King Author Honor, the 2018 Ezra Jack Keats New Writer Award, and the 2018 Kirkus Prize for Young Readers. Derrick is a graduate of Jackson State University and was the first African American male creative copywriter hired by greeting card giant Hallmark Cards.

DAWUD ANYABWILE

is an Emmy Award–winning and two-time Glyph Comics Award–winning comics artist and the founder and CEO of Big City Entertainment. He has received the Key to Kansas City for Outstanding Service to Children and a Lifetime Achievement Award from the East Coast Black Age of Comics Convention. He was nominated for an Eisner Award for Best Artist for his work on the comic series *Brotherman: Dictator of Discipline* and has illustrated books including *Clean Getaway* by Nic Stone, *Becoming Muhammad Ali* by James Patterson and Kwame Alexander, and *Monster* by Walter Dean Myers.